Brimming with creative inspiration, how-to projects, and useful information to enrich your everyday life, Quarto Knows is a favorite destination for those pursuing their interests and passions. Visit our site and dig deeper with our books into your area of interest: Quarto Creates, Quarto Cooks, Quarto Homes, Quarto Lives, Quarto Drives, Quarto Explores, Quarto Gifts, or Quarto Kids.

First published in 2018 by Cool Springs Press,
an imprint of The Quarto Group,
401 Second Avenue North, Suite 310,
Minneapolis, MN 55401 USA.
T (612) 344-8100 F (612) 344-8692
www.QuartoKnows.com

Cool Springs Press titles are also available at discount for retail, wholesale, promotional, and bulk purchase. For details, contact the Special Sales Manager by email at specialsales@quarto.com or by mail at The Quarto Group, Attn: Special Sales Manager, 401 Second Avenue North, Suite 310, Minneapolis, MN 55401 USA.

10 9 8 7 6 5 4 3 2 1

ISBN: 978-0-7603-6079-8

Library of Congress Cataloging-in-Publication Data

Names: Thompson-Adolf, Julie, 1966- author.
Title: Starting & saving seeds : grow the perfect vegetables, fruits, herbs and flowers for your garden / Julie Thompson-Adolf.
Other titles: Starting and saving seeds
Description: Minneapolis, MN : Cool Springs Press, 2018. | Includes index.
Identifiers: LCCN 2018014952 | ISBN 9780760360798 (hc)
Subjects: LCSH: Gardening.
Classification: LCC SB453 .T438 2018 | DDC 635--dc23
LC record available at https://lccn.loc.gov/2018014952

Acquiring Editor: Thom O'Hearn
Project Manager: Alyssa Bluhm
Art Director: Cindy Samargia Laun
Cover and Page Design: Evelin Kasikov
Illustration: Evelin Kasikov
Photography: Libby Williams,
    except as otherwise noted

Printed in China

MIX
Paper from
responsible sources
FSC® C104723

STARTING & SAVING

SEEDS

GROW THE PERFECT VEGETABLES, FRUITS, HERBS, AND FLOWERS FOR YOUR GARDEN

Julie Thompson-Adolf

COOL
SPRINGS
PRESS

PART I

HOW TO START, GROW, AND SAVE SEEDS

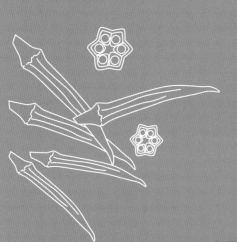

PART II

MEET THE PLANTS

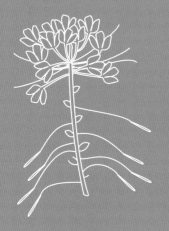

Introduction

When I was in kindergarten, I planted a bean. I imagine at some point as a child you did too. I remember sticking a bean seed in a Dixie cup partially filled with dirt, watering it until the soil became muddy, watching it sprout, then proudly presenting it to my mom and dad. After a week or two of a five-year-old's tough love—*Drown it in water! Carry it everywhere! Tuck it in bed!*—the plant shriveled and died. I hope your little plant enjoyed a happier life than mine.

Often our first, unfortunate experiences growing seeds make us believe we possess black thumbs. I promise you—it's not true. That poor, ill-fated bean simply fell victim to a kindergartener's lack of knowledge about what comes next: how does that cute little sprout turn into a healthy plant that provides pretty blooms and, ultimately, food for a family? My kindergarten teacher, while an incredibly sweet and patient woman, skipped the follow-up lesson.

While some books about seed starting and saving can be a tad technical, that's not the background for most home gardeners. Instead, I believe in an illustrated, learning-by-doing approach. Here you'll find step-by-step instructions for everything from selecting great seeds to creating your own seed-starting mix to harvesting seeds for next year's garden.

I love a good story as much as I adore seeds. Yes, we need to know some science to grow and save seeds properly, but the beauty of heirloom seeds lies not only in the delicious meals we create from our harvests, but also in the history and heritage behind those seeds' origins. Did you know that in the past two hundred years, we've lost 94 percent of the fruit and vegetables that we once grew? I'll introduce you to some of these interesting plant varieties along the way, show how you can grow them in your garden, and help you perpetuate these varieties by saving their seeds.

That said, I'm also the kind of gardener who likes quick recommendations when I'm in a hurry. Let's face it: who among us spends all day, every day, gardening? We want success from our gardens while in the throes of chasing kids, working jobs, and even when writing books. Because daily life interferes with gardening time, I've included highlighted tips throughout the book, such as "Top 10 Tomatoes for Cool, Short-Season Climates" or "Top 10 Prettiest, Tastiest Lettuces."

Think of me as your new friend or the neighbor next door who loves to garden. Together we'll banish any fears of failure and create a beautiful, healthy, delicious, self-sufficient garden—from seed.

Let's get started!

HOW TO START, GROW, AND SAVE SEEDS

CHAPTER 1

Getting Started

In the heart of winter, the seed catalogs arrive. Is there anything better for a gardener's mood than dreaming of beds filled with fruit, vegetables, and blooms? While it's lovely to look through photos and dream of spring, the best part of seed starting is that as the snow still swirls outside your windows, your hands will be buried in seed-starting mix. Sowing seeds and nurturing green babies that will fill your garden is rewarding from the start.

Why Start Seeds?

Seed starting and saving no longer exclusively pertain to farmers and master gardeners. On the contrary, most home gardeners grow something from seed. Whether it's a handful of zinnia seeds sprinkled in a flower bed or a formal potager filled with home-grown flowers, fruits, vegetables, and herbs, seed starting and saving have gained mainstream status among home gardeners in the past decade. If you're like me, there's a tower of seed catalogs on your desk, tempting you with their gorgeous photography and lovely seed stories. Gardeners grow seeds for a variety of reasons. Let's run through a few of them.

Greater Variety

When I started growing plants to sell at our farmers' market, my husband, Peter, was perplexed. "Why do you need to grow sixty-four varieties of tomatoes?" he asked. "Tomatoes are just round and red." Oh, Peter. My poor husband had no idea that two years later, I'd grow 168 varieties of tomatoes in one season.

Red, yellow, black, green, striped, orange, speckled, white . . . why limit yourself to round, red tomatoes? The big box stores and nurseries typically offer only the most basic tomato varieties, and those are mostly hybrid plants. The same is true for cucumbers, beans, peppers, well—really anything you can grow in the garden. Growing from seed opens up a world of colors, flavors, textures, and beauty for your garden. (It's funny. I've realized as I've been harvesting tomatoes this summer, there's not one round, red tomato among the vines. Huh.)

↑ Seeds provide an endless supply of plant varieties. Why settle for red tomatoes when you can grow an entire rainbow of them?

PASSION FOR PURPLE FOOD? GROW THESE UNUSUAL SEEDS

- 'Purple Podded' Pole Bean
- 'Cherokee Purple' Tomato
- 'Purple Beauty' Bell Pepper
- 'Black Beauty' Eggplant
- 'Violetta Italia' Cauliflower
- 'Purple Dragon' Carrot
- 'Early Purple Sprouting' Broccoli
- 'Tête Noire' Cabbage
- 'Early Purple Vienna' Kohlrabi
- Blue Podded Blauwschokkers Peas

← Starting seeds allows you to skip the big box stores. Instead, seed starting lets you grow healthy plants, perfectly timed for your garden.

Better Control

When you grow plants from seeds, you're in greater control of when to start your crops of food and flowers. Yes, you'll need a bit of planning and some extra resources to outsmart Mother Nature and get a jump on the growing season. Still, it's worth it to have healthy, mature transplants ready to plant after the danger of frost is past. And if you own a greenhouse, growing from seed allows you to grow delicious food and lovely blooms all year long. Even if you don't have the budget for a greenhouse, you can still benefit from plants grown from seed year-round, with a little creativity.

Likewise, you're in better control of the health of your plants. We've all seen transplants at certain stores that look less than well-tended. Besides the droopy leaves from lack of water or the obvious heat stress, are you confident that those organic vegetable plants are truly organic? Did a part-time worker accidentally dose them with pesticide? If you're growing flowers for pollinators, the last thing you want is a plant grown with neonicotinoids—insecticides absorbed by plants, which can then transfer to its pollen and nectar. As you can imagine, if you're growing flowers to attract pollinators, you don't want to offer them a toxic buffet. By growing your own plants from seed, you know that the plants going into your garden—and into your dinner—are healthy.

Save Money and Make Money

Growing and saving seeds should help your budget. For instance, I used to purchase annuals for my front beds. Each flat cost $17.99 for thirty-two plants. Do you think I bought one flat of plants? Of course not. Imagine how many flats of plants you can grow from a $2 pack of seeds instead. Plus, most seeds are viable for several years. Your first pack of tomato seeds may last four or five years. Then, you'll have your own tomatoes that will produce seeds to save for future garden seasons. Very economical!

There is a bit of expense involved in setting up a seed-starting operation, but you'll use your tools for years. Plus, I'll share inexpensive DIY projects to minimize your start-up expenses.

Seed starting can also generate income. When I began my seed-starting adventures, I grew so many organic heirloom tomato, pepper, and herb starts that I began selling the extra plants at my community farmers' market. The next year, I turned my seed obsession into a full-blown business, selling plants online as well. While selling organic transplants will never make you a billionaire, it's a great way to make a little money doing something you love. Plus, I adored selling at our farmers' market. I met many terrific people who were excited to learn how to grow their own food and flowers.

Connect with History and Other Cultures

Reading about history is great, but growing history is even better. Heirloom seeds tell stories. From obscure family seeds passed down through generations to the well-known stories of "Trail of Tears" beans that survived the Cherokee people's forced displacement in 1839, seeds bring history to life.

Additionally, growing from seed gives you access to international foods and flavors from your garden. Perhaps you loved a particular tomato variety in a country where you grew up, or maybe your parents created delicious dishes with ingredients you can't find in traditional grocery stores. Growing food from seed allows you to add those favorite vegetables, fruit, and herbs to your garden so you can recreate the comforts of home.

↑ Starting seeds allows you to grow the food you love, connecting with other cultures or your family's food history.

Emotional Satisfaction from Start to Finish

For most gardeners, the gray days of winter make us a little crazy. I itch to get my hands in the soil. So, what do I do when the first snow falls? I pull out the seed catalogs and dream of spring. As the mailbox fills with manila envelopes stuffed with seed orders, I'm anxious to start growing. Armed with a list of seeds, their germination timing, and my last frost dates, I calculate when to start sowing and decide—it's time! Get the seed trays ready, throw off the gray weather gloom. Let's make some green babies! The beauty of seed starting is that, as snow swirls outside, I can rightfully play in the soil, filling trays, planting seeds, and tending tiny green seedlings. Seed starting offers a bit of joy during ugly winter days for many gardeners.

Now skip to the end of the journey. You'll find there's an amazing sense of pride when all the ingredients for a meal you cooked, or even just the starring vegetable, began life as tiny seeds that you sowed. Then you pampered, transplanted, coddled, watered, watched, harvested, prepped, and finally cooked them for dinner. "Yep, this ratatouille began with seeds I planted in January!"

↑ Creating meals from plants you've grown is incredibly satisfying—and economical too.

↑ Black, white, tiny, large, colorful . . . seeds are nature's artwork, packed with goodness inside.

Botany 101: A Quick Overview of Seeds

When you open a seed packet and spill out its contents, what do you see? From tiny, sandlike grains of poppy seeds to oblong, flat pumpkin seeds, what you're really looking at is potential. No matter the size or shape, inside every seed is a living plant just waiting to spring into action.

Sure, it's embryonic, but the life within a seed possesses all the necessary elements to grow into a strong, beautiful, productive plant. It's simply waiting for the right conditions to realize its potential. Until the environment presents the perfect factors, the future plant within a seed behaves as plants do. It carries on respiration, absorbing oxygen and releasing carbon dioxide. It takes in water from the air, allowing it to convert stored carbohydrates into food. It thrives within its seed coat until the conditions are perfect for it to realize its promise—and germinate.

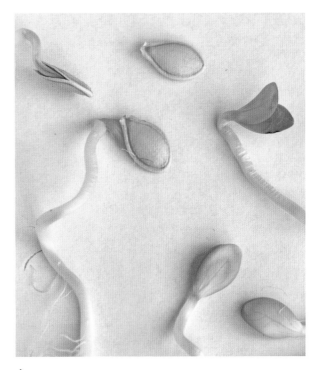

↑ Every seed is alive, waiting for the right conditions to grow.

↑ Most seeds fall into the dicot category, which have two cotyledon, but seeds in the grass family are monocots.

Now, let's think back to the good old days when we tried desperately to stay awake in biology class. (I know my fourteen-year-old self never imagined I'd actually need and use this information one day.) Remember those lessons about cotyledons, dicots, and monocots? Well, now you can see them in action.

Inside the seed case, you'll find *cotyledons*, also known as the seed leaves. A cotyledon attaches to the root tip and surrounds the tiny leaf bud. The cotyledon functions to absorb and, in some cases, store food for the embryo produced from the surrounding starchy tissue. All seeds, regardless of size or shape, contain a cotyledon (one or two), stem, leafy bud, and root tip.

Monocots contain one cotyledon. Think of plants in the grass family (Gramineae), like cereal crops. In most of these plants, food is stored in the seed at the time of germination, and the single cotyledon continues to absorb nutrients and pass them on to the rest of the seedling until it can photosynthesize.

Dicots possess two cotyledons. In most dicots, which include vegetable seedlings and flowering plants, the cotyledons absorb all the nutrients in the seed by the time germination occurs. Some cotyledons continue to feed the seedling until it can photosynthesize; then they shrivel and drop off. Others turn green and start to photosynthesize themselves. This is why teachers use beans in experiments. Beans provide the perfect examples of dicots with their two, relatively large cotyledons wrapped around the tiny embryo. The cotyledons make a great show as they unfurl during germination, much to the wonder of children.

In some seeds, the stored food source isn't the cotyledon. Instead, a layer called the *endosperm* surrounds the embryo, feeding the seed. From the time it matures on the parent plant until it breaks dormancy in the next growing season, the endosperm provides sustenance for the seed. In certain cases, such as sweet corn, the endosperm is the food we humans enjoy from the plant. Just make sure to set aside some seeds to grow the next season! The perfect little powerhouse package that will eventually become a fabulous flower or tasty tomato remains dormant, biding its time, until conditions are ideal for it to break dormancy. (We'll talk about how to make that happen in chapter 3.)

WHERE CAN YOU FIND SEEDS?

- Seed catalogs
- Online seed stores and nurseries
- Seed swaps, local and online
- Independent garden centers
- Seed-saving organizations
- Family heirlooms
- Friends with gardens
- Your garden
- Seed libraries
- Nature (but never take seeds from nature preserves or botanical gardens without permission)

← Take a close look at your space before placing your garden. If you want to grow food and flowers, you'll need 6–8 hours of sunlight each day for a productive garden.

Planning Your Garden

Now that we've had a quick seed anatomy review, let's start planning the seed-starting adventure. Before you begin growing dozens of tomatoes or planting pretty poppies, take an objective look at your growing space. Then look at it again. And again. Walk outside, noting the amount of sunlight your garden receives in the morning, at noon, and in late afternoon. Then look at your garden at the same times in each season. (Yes, even in winter, particularly if you intend to grow in a moderate climate or under protective coverings.)

It's important to note the amount of sun your garden receives, doubly so if you want to grow plants that require six to eight hours of sunlight, like many vegetables, fruits, and flowers. The worst thing to do is invest hours, days, weeks, and even months growing

gorgeous, strong, healthy seedlings—only to plant them in the wrong garden conditions. It's frustrating for you and certain death for your green babies.

You'll also want to make sure you'll have easy access to a water source to keep your plants hydrated. If you live in a wet climate or have wet parts on your property, check to ensure your garden location isn't too soggy. (To check the soil's moisture, dig a hole in the area 6 to 8 inches [15 to 20 cm] deep, then scoop a handful of soil into your palm. Squeeze the soil. If the soil crumbles without forming a ball, it's too dry. If the ball remains firm even when prodded, the soil is too wet. If it forms a ball that easily falls apart when touched, the soil's moisture level is ideal.) Choose a location that contains rich, well-drained soil—or build raised beds and add a mix of nutrient-rich compost and soil as needed. Prepare the garden space by removing weeds, as they'll compete with seedlings for water and nutrients.

Once you have your site, consider your space and plan accordingly. One indeterminate tomato plant can reach more than 6 feet high and sprawl 3 feet wide—even when it's staked. You don't need acreage to grow successfully but you do need to pick the right plants for the space. Smaller tomato varieties can grow well in a container on a patio, for instance. Check your seed packets to determine the space requirements of the mature plants.

Finally, if possible, choose a site where you can enjoy the fruits of your labor. A space close to the kitchen is excellent if you're growing food or herbs to use when preparing dinner. A bed in front of your office window will provide a great view of your lovely cutting garden that you grew from seed, with a bouquet from it used to brighten your desk. And a space filled with homegrown *Echinacea* outside your family room can provide endless hours of fun as you watch bees, butterflies, and birds enjoying the pollen, nectar, and seeds of your labor. (Just make sure to save some seeds for next year before the finches eat them all!)

What to Grow?

Before you order the first seed pack, decide if you want to grow food, flowers, or a combination. I'm a believer in companion planting—the practice of planting beneficial flowers and herbs among food crops to deter pests and attract pollinators. I always add many flower packets to my seed orders.

Once you decide what kind of garden you want to grow, make a list. If you want to grow flowers for your landscape, what colors and textures complement your home? If you desire beautiful bouquets to grace

← Even if you're a die-hard vegetable lover, adding flowers to your garden helps encourage pollination of your crops. Plus, they add beauty to the beds.

your dining room table, make a list of your favorite flowers, but also include filler plants to grow that can add to those bouquets too. If you're growing an edibles garden, make a list of your favorite foods and ask members of your family to do the same. I can assure you, my youngest son would be delighted if I'd cross yellow crookneck squash off my growing list. Also, if you're looking to stretch your budget by growing a home garden from seed, consider growing some of the more expensive produce. Organic peppers, kale, swiss chard, artichokes, strawberries—these can all be easily started from seed.

A word of caution: If this is your first year growing from seed, start small to avoid feeling overwhelmed. Pick a few of your very favorite flowers or food crops to grow from seed. Seed starting can be time consuming and frustrating if you're trying to grow too many plants while learning the basics.

There's plenty of time to grow 168 varieties of heirloom tomatoes next year.

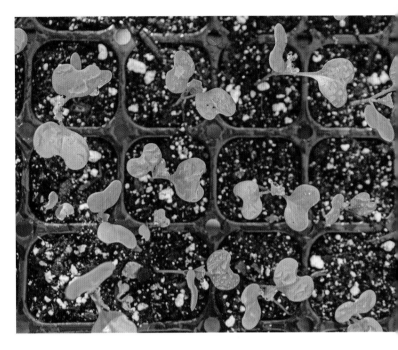

↑ Choosing the types of seeds you grow is a personal decision—but remember, to save seeds from your plants, you'll need to grow open-pollinated varieties.

Seed Terminology

Before we discuss the different "flavors" of seeds available, let's dispel one common misconception. Although there's much media attention and debate about genetically modified seeds, also known as GMO seeds, home gardeners are not sold GMO seeds. Unless you're a farmer who signs an agreement with a company that produces GMO seeds, GMO seeds won't cross your path. They're not available to home gardeners. So, when you're trying to decide what seeds to grow, know that any seed sold to you, the home gardener, is GMO free.

Whew. Feel better? Seed shopping can be confusing though. Let's clarify a few terms about the types of seeds available for your garden.

Open-pollinated: Open-pollinated seeds derive from plants in which pollination occurs by insects, birds, wind,

humans, or other natural sources. Plants pollinated within the same species will produce seeds genetically true to type and that are similar to the parent plant.

Heirloom: The definition of an heirloom seed varies in the gardening community. Some people assign an age to a plant, stating that it's not an heirloom unless it's been grown in cultivation for more than 50 years. However, I prefer the definition that links the plant and its seed to heritage and history. Many gardeners consider a plant as an heirloom if it's historically linked to a family, community, or region. Heirloom plants are also open-pollinated, meaning the mature seed can be saved and grown to produce a plant that's true to its parents. Helping to conserve biodiversity and providing an historical food connection makes heirloom seeds a popular choice. Personally, heirlooms are my favorite type of seeds because I love the stories they tell.

Hybrids: Some people I know give hybrids a bad rap, equating them to GMOs. Hybrid seeds have nothing to do with GMOs, and many hybrids occur naturally in the garden through random cross-pollination. Plant breeders work to select desired traits from different parent plants to create new, improved varieties. These traits might include higher yields, greater disease resistance, or shorter vines, for instance. However, seeds saved and grown from a hybrid plant prove unstable: they do not grow true to the parent plant. A gardener needs to purchase new hybrid seeds each year.

While my garden is 98 percent heirloom and open-pollinated plants, I always grow a few hybrids as well, particularly squash. In the heat and humidity in my climate, I need a squash that withstands fungus and resists squash vine borers. Plus, I typically add shorter vining crops and flowers to containers, placing them around my pool or along our front walkway. I grow containers filled with edibles and flowers wherever I can find a bit of sun. Many hybrid varieties were created to grow in smaller spaces, like containers, allowing land-challenged gardeners to benefit from crops in pots.

Organic Versus Conventional Seeds

Ultimately, buying organic is a personal decision. If seed is labeled "organic," you can be confident that the grower passed a rigorous screening process to achieve that certification. The main thing to know is that organic seeds are harvested from plants that are free from conventional chemical pesticides, herbicides, and nonorganic fertilizers. Conventional seeds can come from any plant grown under any method, including the use of chemical fertilizers, insecticides, and fungicides.

That said, I also know farmers who grow using organic practices but who don't have the time and money necessary to undergo the certification process. It's cumbersome and expensive for a smaller grower. Knowing these growers, I trust that their seeds are organic. Likewise, there have been times I've purchased conventional seeds for plants when I can't find organic sources, and then raised the plants organically. It's not perfect, but sometimes I really, really need to grow an unusual seed and can't find an organic source.

- -

WHERE TO FIND THE BEST HYBRID SEEDS

While I'm a believer in heirloom, open-pollinated plants, I'm also a believer that sometimes you need a little help in the garden. If you're constantly plagued by squash vine borer or your tomatoes succumb to disease every year, hybrid seeds may help alleviate your garden woes. My favorite source for hybrid seeds is an organization that carefully trials and selects the best new varieties: All-America Selections (AAS). I've toured their plant trials, and for someone who is a vigorous supporter of heirloom seeds, I've added several AAS winners to my garden. While you won't want to save seeds from hybrids, as most hybrid seeds do not grow true to their parent plants, it is worth investing in these seeds each year if you have trouble spots in your garden. (And honestly? There are some AAS Winner snapdragons that I grow because they're incredibly beautiful.) In Europe, the AAS counterpart is Fleuroselect, while in Japan, the organization is Japan Flower Selection (JFS).

. N O T E .

If you are planting flowers for pollinators, please avoid pesticides, conventional or organic—the wildlife will thank you. If you're struggling with diseases or pests in your garden, there are many outstanding organic options to try before using a synthetic chemical approach.

← When planting for pollinators, please keep the flowers pesticide-free. Even organic pesticides can harm pollinators.

Further to the organic discussion, certain seeds, such as peas, tend to rot in unfavorable conditions or "damp off" (which occurs when a seedling dies due to fungal issues). To avoid poor germination rates, some companies apply a chemical coating to the seeds, which typically contains antifungal or antibacterial chemicals to improve germination success. Obviously, these treated seeds are not organic.

Timing the Seed-Starting Process

As exciting as a fresh pile of seed packets might be when they arrive in the dead of winter, sometimes the early bird ends up disappointed, at least where seed starting is concerned. Start seeds too early, and you can end up with leggy, overgrown plants that need babying until frost disappears and the garden warms. Start seeds too late, and you'll be drooling over your neighbor's BLTs while forlornly willing your plants' blooms to turn into fruit. So, how does a gardener know when it's prime time to start seeds?

First, find out your last frost date in the spring if you're planting warm-weather crops. If you're planting cool-weather crops, you need to know the first expected freeze date for the fall. (A great resource that shows frost dates throughout the world is found at www.plantsmap.com.) After you're armed with frost date knowledge, you can determine when to begin seeds, based on information found on your seed packet. Some seed packets are a wealth of information—others, not so much. No worries. Chapters 4 and 5 provide detailed information for optimal seed-starting times, as well as dates to maturity per seed variety.

Now that we've covered the basics of planning the seed-starting adventure, let's gather our supplies.

CHAPTER 2

Starting Seeds

Seeds are magical. From growing culturally important food conserved through Slow Food's Ark of Taste to the pure pleasure of poppies, seeds offer connections to people, culture, and the earth. There's so much potential packed into a tiny seed.

Before beginning a seed-starting adventure, it's helpful to consider the environment that's best for growing seeds. In this chapter, I'll share the supplies I use so you can gather them and prepare for the uninterrupted bliss of seed starting. Then, I'll hold your hand—virtually, but you can imagine that I'm right beside you— so you can successfully start your seeds.

Are you excited? Let's do this!

Indoor Seed Starting

The first year that I grew plants to sell at our farmers' market, my basement and garage were overrun with plants on utility shelves, sitting under shop lights. I'm surprised that our neighbors didn't report me, because the glow emanating from the garage looked a little shady. (I imagined the neighbors peeking at our house saying, "What *are* those Adolfs growing over there? Do we need to call the police?") While the then-unfinished basement worked well for the seedlings, it proved to be a constant battle to regulate the temperature in the garage. When setting up your seed starting station, consider the needs of your plants—and your sanity.

PLANTS REQUIRE:

- Adequate light
- Controlled temperatures
- Access to water
- Good airflow

YOUR SANITY REQUIRES:

- Mess that's out of sight
- Easy clean-up
- Comfortable work station
- Access to electricity

↑ Make yourself comfortable. It's time to start seeds.

PRACTICAL VERSUS PRETTY

Perhaps you're fortunate to own a lovely little greenhouse that's perfect for seed starting. Lucky you! However, for most gardeners, seed-starting operations are squeezed into basements, dining rooms, playrooms—wherever space allows. It's important to realize that seeds will become a permanent part of your décor (at least until spring arrives).

To minimize the mess if you're growing inside your home, spread out plastic or an absorbent, washable blanket under your work station for easy spillage clean up.

An old table and chair downstairs served as my potting bench. Now that I've graduated to a greenhouse, I use an easily cleaned, 6-foot-long folding table, where I sit to sow the seeds in trays and pot up seedlings into larger containers.

Remember, when you see photos online or in magazines of darling seedlings sitting on a windowsill in the kitchen, that's not reality. The seedlings will stretch awkwardly toward the light, growing leggy and weak. Ditto for the cute photos of seedlings sprouting in eggshells. Those unhappy seedlings look

adorable for about a week, and then they suffer from inadequate soil and moisture. You want beautiful, healthy seedlings that will grow into beautiful, healthy, productive plants in your garden. A black plastic propagation tray or recycled plastic produce container from the grocery store may not look Instagram-worthy, but you'll produce healthy, happy plants. Strong, healthy seedlings are the first step to a bountiful harvest. And that's the goal, right?

Once you decide where your seed-starting station will be located, it's time to gather your supplies.

← If you want healthy plants, make sure you give them proper light. A windowsill isn't adequate.

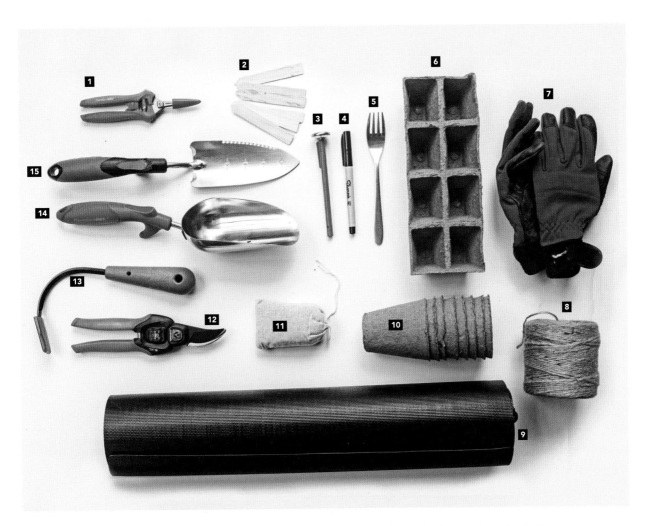

↑ Gather your supplies. **1** snips **2** plant tags **3** soil thermometer **4** marker **5** fork **6** biodegradable seed cells **7** garden gloves **8** twine **9** heat mat **10** biodegradable plant pots **11** compost tea bag **12** hand pruners **13** Cobra-head weeder **14** soil scoop **15** transplanting trowel with a serrated edge

Supplies

Before you begin sowing seeds, it's helpful to organize your supplies. Seed starting can be messy, and I hate stopping midway through because I forgot plant tags or a marker and need to search for them. Once I'm in my seed-starting Zen, I like to stay in my happy place instead of cursing my missing marker.

The beauty of seed starting is that many recycled—or upcycled—containers make terrific homes for seedlings. Whether it's a container for rotisserie chicken (it provides a perfect mini-greenhouse effect) or recyclable plastic strawberry containers from the grocery store (the slits in the bottom provide good drainage, and the top mimics the domes of seed trays), you'll find many options by sorting through your recycling bin or refrigerator.

↑ Recycled paper towel tubes make perfect biodegradable seedling pots.

↑ Propagation trays come in a range of cell counts. Use small cells for plants such as lettuce, which will be transplanted quickly, and larger cells for plants that grow deep root systems.

A word of caution: Make sure that whatever you choose to use for growing seedlings offers plenty of depth for adequate growing mix. You want strong, big roots, and they can't develop in a tiny bit of growing medium or space. Additionally, if the container doesn't have drainage holes, cut some into the bottom. Finally, avoid water damage on furniture by placing the recycled containers with drainage holes on a solid tray. Even an old baking sheet with a rim works well to contain overflow.

Also, while saving money by growing a garden from seed is a fabulous goal, a few purchases when you're beginning the seed-starting journey will make your adventure a bit easier and more enjoyable. Consider these items as investments; most supplies will last for years. What follows are my recommendations.

- Seed-starting germination flats that fit into solid trays: I prefer the 128-cell flats, as I can grow a lot of seeds in little space. Plus, four of these trays fit perfectly on one large heat mat when arranged side-by-side vertically. Four trays also fit under the seed-starting light station, which I'll show you how to build on page 28. The solid bottom tray allows you to water plants from below so that tiny seedlings aren't disturbed.

- Clear acrylic domes (for propagation trays): The domes help retain moisture and warmth for young seedlings. You'll remove the domes as the plants grow.

- 4-foot shop lights: Save money and avoid buying light fixtures marketed for "seed starting." Inexpensive shop lights work perfectly well. I use two double-light fixtures hung side by side to ensure the plants receive adequate light.

- Full-spectrum fluorescent light bulbs. Again, save money and buy fluorescent light bulbs ranging from 4,000 to 6,000 Kelvin, which mimics natural outdoor daylight. There's no need to purchase more expensive plant lights.

- Timer for lights

- Zip ties: Use these to attach the lights to the grow station or to chains, depending on your light frame. (They're also useful to contain multiple electric cords.)

- Adjustable chains and S hooks: Attach them to lights, allowing you to raise and lower the lights. (Chains often are included with the light fixtures.) You'll need four S hooks per light to attach the chains to light fixtures and the seed-starting station frame.

- Heat mat for seed starting: Invest in one that's waterproof and intended for seed starting. Don't cut corners here and use a heating pad because you risk electrocution. Trays leak and water spills. Buy a waterproof heat mat. They're perfect for tricky seeds that require bottom heat, like tomatoes and peppers, and they speed germination time for many other seeds. Look for a heat mat with a soil temperature sensor attachment that regulates heat settings. (You don't want to bake your seeds.)

- Spray bottle

- Large container: Buy one for mixing and storing seed-starting mix plus another for potting soil; I prefer large storage containers with lids. I combine the seed-starting mix ingredients, moisten the mix with water, and easily scoop the mix into trays—with the tray balanced over the container, ensuring any spilled soil ends up back in the container—and then place the lid on it for storage. I use another container for potting soil. It's much easier than scooping soil from a bag, and it stores well in the container.

- Thermometer: You'll need one to monitor air temperature. If you're growing in a greenhouse, I highly recommend a temperature sensor tied to an app that shows the current greenhouse temperature on your smartphone, alerting you to variances. (I learned the hard way when my greenhouse overheated and killed five thousand plants. Don't be me.)

- Plant tags: Small wooden craft popsicle sticks or plastic plant markers work well. There are many options for labeling plants but make certain the label will fit under the acrylic humidity dome if you're using germination trays.

- Permanent marker or grease pencil

- Containers with drainage holes: use these to pot up seedlings. I use biodegradable pots that can be planted straight into the garden.

- Shovel or cup to scoop soil

- Seed-starting mix

- Potting soil

- Dinner fork

- Extension cord and/or power strip: You'll want this to power-up lights and heat mats easily.

- 5-gallon bucket

- Compost tea bag

- Watering can

MAKE YOUR OWN SEED-STARTING MIX

While it's easy to purchase a good, balanced commercial seed-starting mix, it's also easy and less expensive to make your own mix, especially if you plan to grow many seeds.

My favorite formula includes equal parts of each of the following:

- **Vermiculite,** which is mica that's been exposed to extreme heat. It absorbs water and nutrients from fertilizers, releasing them gradually to benefit the seedling.

- **Peat moss or fine sphagnum moss,** which supports the plant and promotes good root development.

- **Perlite,** or expanded volcanic ash, which promotes good drainage.

Combine. Depending on how much you need, you might use a 5-gallon bucket of each ingredient, or you may need only two cups of each. Mix the ingredients together well in a container, then add warm water to moisten the mix thoroughly, making certain it isn't soggy. I dig in with my hands, squeezing the water through the mix. It's best to add water a few hours before you want to fill seed trays, as it takes a while for the mix to fully absorb the water. Now you're ready to fill the trays!

↑ Peat moss (left), vermiculite (center), and perlite (right) are easy to combine into an inexpensive seed-starting mix.

The Indoor Seed-Starting Station

Because I grow so many seeds each year, I use a variety of seed-starting stations. Their common traits include that they're all sturdy, located in an area with good airflow and temperature controls, placed where nothing important can be damaged, have easy access to water, and contain a light source. I can also raise and lower the lights as the plants grow. I use 4-foot-long (122 cm) shop lights with two fluorescent bulbs purchased from a hardware store. They're inexpensive, easy to adjust, and provide a good light source for up to four trays of plants placed side by side. The lights mimic the sun, offering a full color spectrum for strong plant growth.

My seed-starting stations vary a bit though; several frames are built from recycled lumber. One is an inexpensive, four-shelf mini greenhouse I ordered online; one is a small station built from scrap metal and a piece of leftover wood; and the last is an inexpensive alternative created with PVC pipe and connectors. Of course, there are plenty of pricy light systems and seed-starting stations available through gardening supply stores and online. However, I've found that as soon as you search the internet for "gardening seed starting lights," the price doubles compared to other, more practical and equally productive options. I'm not the handiest person with power tools, but even I built a PVC seed-starting station without issues. You can too.

SUPPLIES

(2) 10' (305 cm) length, 1" (3 cm) PVC pipe
(4) 1" (3 cm) PVC end-caps
(4) 1" (3 cm) PVC tees
(4) 1" (3 cm) PVC elbows
Zip ties

↑ Build an inexpensive seed-starting light station to give your seedlings the best start in life.

Directions

1 Cut one 10' (305 cm) PVC pipe into the following lengths using a hack saw or PVC cutter: (4) 5" (13 cm) lengths; (2) 24" (61 cm) lengths; (1) 52" (131 cm) length.

2 Cut the second 10' (305 cm) PVC pipe into the following lengths: (2) 7.5" (19 cm) lengths; (2) 24" (61 cm) lengths; (1) 52" (131 cm) length. (You'll have a bit left over.)

3 Place one end-cap on a 5" (13 cm) section of PVC pipe. Insert the other end into a PVC tee. Repeat three times.

4 Insert one 7.5" (19 cm) PVC pipe into other ends of tee, joining the 5" (13 cm) sections. Repeat.

5 Insert one 24" (61 cm) length into PVC tee top. Repeat three times.

6 Attach an elbow to each end of the 52" (131 cm) pipe, with the bend facing downward.

7 Join the two 24" (61 cm) length pipes into the open ends of the elbows. Repeat. The frame should stand alone without support. You may need to straighten the pipes or connectors slightly.

8 Add zip ties a few inches from each end of the 52" (131 cm) pipe to attach chains for the lights.

9 Hang the lights 1" (3 cm) above the plants. Adjust the chain to raise the lights as plants grow.

10 Plug the lights into a power strip and plug the power strip into the timer.

11 Set the timer so plants receive 12–14 hours of light per day.

12 Disassemble pipes/connectors for storage.

Timing and Other Considerations

You've selected the seeds. You've built a seed-starting station and gathered your supplies. Now the fun begins! But wait—before you break out the trays and open the seed packets, there's one very important issue to consider: timing.

Start too early, and your poor seedlings will outgrow their indoor homes, becoming cramped in containers and potentially malnourished without adequate food. Start too late, and you'll be eyeing your neighbors' tomatoes enviously while awaiting your first tomato blooms. Plus, planting large transplants can be cumbersome, as plants with fragile stems, like peppers, can snap more easily. So, when is the perfect time to start seeds? It depends. Here are the primary considerations.

Warm- versus cold-season crops: Different crops are planted at different times of the year. *Brassica* species, like broccoli, prefer cool temperatures and bolt in the heat. Tomatoes need warm weather and can't tolerate frost. For instance, the last frost date in my area is typically April 15. Knowing that tomatoes, peppers, and eggplants need 6 to 8 weeks to grow prior to transplanting into the garden, I'll start those seeds around February 15. You don't have to memorize anything though. Chapters 4 and 5 will tell you approximately when to start seeds of various plants based on the days to maturity.

Gardening zones: First and last frost dates depend upon geography. You can find your area's projected first and last frost dates online. Warm-weather crops need to be planted after any chance of frost has passed.

Germination rates: Some seeds germinate more quickly than others, and plants grow at different rates. Seed-starting timing depends on an individual plant's traits.

Special considerations: Many seeds require special prepping to encourage germination. Factor in extra time if the seeds require stratification, soaking, or scarification (for more, see sidebar).

SPECIAL CONSIDERATIONS FOR CHALLENGING SEEDS

Some seeds need extra encouragement to germinate. These prima donnas require more effort on your part, but the results are usually worth it. Plant descriptions in chapters 4 and 5 tell which plants require special coaxing for germination. Three methods to encourage germination include:

Scarification: A seed with a thick coat can be impenetrable to moisture or gases that trigger germination. In nature, an animal might eat a seed, and its digestive juices break down the seed coat before it passes. Freezing temperatures or microbial activities can also help weaken a tough coating. However, it's easy to mimic nature and encourage germination. Just like the name implies, you'll "scar" the seed coat. Using a nail file, sandpaper, or a knife, scratch or nick the seed coat, which will allow the seed to absorb water and begin germination. Be careful though— only remove a bit of the coating without injuring the interior of the seed.

Stratification: For seeds that require a chilling period before germination, like some perennials, all you need is a refrigerator and a bag or container filled with perlite, vermiculite, sand, or seed-starting mix. (Mark the seed variety name on the bag.) Moisten the mix, add the seeds, and place in the refrigerator, not the freezer. Stratification requirements vary by species. Some plants prefer 2 weeks of cold treatment, some require 2 months or longer. Regardless of the length, never let the seeds dry out during stratification.

Soaking: A 24-hour bath in lukewarm water encourages certain seeds with a wrinkled appearance, such as nasturtium, to absorb water and begin germination. I soak many seed varieties to give them a little germination boost before I plant.

← ↑ ↑ Some seeds are more challenging than others and need scarification, stratification, or soaking to boost germination.

How to Plant Seeds Indoors

You've checked the weather, and you know your first and last frost dates. Using chapters 4 and 5 as your reference, you've stratified your seeds, researched their germination rates, know which seeds prefer bottom heat and which need light to germinate, and you've made a plan of when to start. The time is here. Finally, it's time to start your seeds!

1 Start by filling your containers or seed germination cells/trays with moistened seed-starting mix.

2 Using your index finger, firm the mix into the cell/container, leaving a shallow indentation.

3 Place one or two seeds per cell/container (depending on the size of the container, you may add more seeds, but don't overcrowd).

4 Using chapters 4 and 5 as a reference, either cover seeds with seed-starting mix (depending on how deeply the seeds should be sown) or cover with just a dusting of mix. Some seeds require dark for germination, others need light. All of them will require light once seedlings emerge.

5 Using a spray bottle, gently water the seeds to settle them.

6 Place the trays on a heat mat, if required, and insert the heat sensor into the soil.

7 Cover the tray with acrylic dome/clear plastic wrap/baggie to maintain moisture and warmth.

8 Turn on the grow lights and adjust the light fixture so that it's 1" (3 cm) above the seeds. Adjust the timer so that plants receive 12–16 hours of light per day.

9 Monitor daily and water as needed. Do not let the seeds dry out. If you're using germination cells inserted into a solid tray, add water into the bottom of the tray, allowing the cells to absorb it as needed. This also avoids disturbing newly planted seeds/young seedlings.

10 As seeds begin to germinate, the first leaves to appear will be the cotyledon. Continue to water as needed.

11 Remove the humidity dome as the plants grow, to allow good airflow.

12 If you've planted too any seeds per cell/container, thin them to allow the strongest to grow well. Remove stunted seedlings and those with weak stems or poor root systems, as they're less likely to thrive.

13 As the first true leaves appear, it's time to move the seedlings into a bigger home.

14 Prepare to transplant. (See page 41 for more on transplanting.)

Direct Sowing

For those gardeners in temperate climates, direct sowing can be a timesaving option. Think of farmers, plowing neat rows to sow seeds each season. Direct sowing also works for specific crops in your garden, particularly ones that don't like their roots disturbed, such as corn or radishes.

In my garden, I mix direct sowing and indoor seed starting, starting seeds for crops that require a longer germination period or consistent heat. I also start some seeds for our potager, as I like to control the planting design. Direct sowing tends to be more challenging when creating an orderly potager or perfectly arranged garden, because seeds can scatter due to a heavy rainstorm, visiting wildlife, or other factors—say rogue chickens that decide to dust bathe in beds right after you finish sowing seeds.

However, direct sowing provides big benefits.

- **It saves space:** There's no need for an elaborate seed-starting station indoors.

- **It saves money:** There are no extra supplies needed, like peat pots or grow lights.

- **It saves time:** There's no need to "pot up" or transplant when seeds are directly grown in the garden.

DIRECT SOWING SUPPLIES

- Seeds
- Wooden or metal stakes and string (optional)
- Measuring tape or ruler
- Trowel or garden hoe for making rows
- Plant tags
- Permanent marker/grease pencil/paint pen

How to Direct Sow Seeds

Direct sowing is easy. As with indoor seed starting, you'll want to do your research first, figuring out your last frost date for summer crops and timing your seed starting based on the plants' requirements. Also, using chapters 4 and 5, determine each variety's planting depth, light requirements, and spacing needs. Only then is it time to start planting!

As you scout the location where you'll plant, make certain your garden bed is free from rocks or roots that might impede seed growth, as well as free from weeds so that your plants can avoid competition for nutrients and water.

→ When the weather warms, is there anything nicer than sowing seeds in the garden?

If you're finicky about garden neatness and order, I highly recommend using two stakes with a string tied to each stake. Insert one stake at the end of the row you intend to plant and stretch the string to the end of the row, then insert the second stake. Use the guide to create a straight planting row with a hoe or trowel, digging the row to accommodate the seeds' required depths. Space seeds according to the plants' requirements, and cover with soil. Water gently to settle the soil and seeds; label the row with plant markers.

To create another row, use the measuring tape to measure based on the recommended spacing distance from the first row to begin a new row. Insert another stake to mark the new row. Measure again at the end of the first row and insert a stake at the end of the new row to ensure even spacing and a straight line. Continue creating rows and adding seeds as space allows.

Another way to achieve a neat, orderly line is by using a seed tape. Commercial seed tapes can be costly, and I've also found only limited seed varieties are available. Instead, during the winter months when I'm anxious to do something garden-related, I make my own seed tapes. It's easy and inexpensive, and you can enlist your friends, significant other, or children to help. It's also a handy way to manage tiny seeds, like basil, which I always sow too thickly in the garden. If you'd like to make your own seed tapes, see page 35.

Once the seeds are in the ground, you'll want to check the garden daily for plant germination. Thin crowded seedlings as needed and ensure there's adequate water. (I stick my index finger an inch into the soil. If it's dry, I water.)

Seed Tape

When you're anxious to garden but the snow swirls outside, making seed tapes is an ideal activity to get a jump on the gardening season. Sitting comfortably in a chair and spacing the seeds on paper while listening to music or chatting with family beats squatting over

↑ Use two stakes and a piece of twine as a guide to make straight lines when direct sowing.

a raised bed in the cold and sowing too many seeds— only to eventually thin them due to overcrowding. When the weather warms, you're ready to go: lay the seed tape flat in the garden bed, cover with soil, and water. Direct sowing—done!

4   Using tweezers or your fingers, place a single seed on each glue dot. Continue until the length of paper is complete.

5   Fold the other half of the toilet paper over the seeds and allow the glue to dry.

6   Once completely dry, roll or fold the seed tape and place in a bag or envelope to store.

7   Mark the seed variety on the outside of the container.

8   Store in a cool, dry place until planting time. (Check seed variety viability in chapters 4 and 5 to determine maximum storage length.)

SUPPLIES

- 60 seeds, spaced 1" (3 cm) apart (check spacing requirements for the variety you wish to plant, and adjust accordingly)

- (15) 4" (10 cm) toilet paper squares, attached, approximately 5' long (1.5 m) (single ply is fine)

- Nontoxic glue, like Elmer's

- 1 zippered plastic storage bag or a large paper envelope, for each seed tape variety

- Marker

Directions

1   On a large, flat surface, unroll a length of toilet paper. (Because toilet paper can tear easily, I like to work in segments. My raised beds are 10 feet long, so I make my seed tapes 5 feet long and use two seed tapes per row. Use whatever length is appropriate for your garden.)

2   Fold the toilet paper in half length-wise, making a crease, then unfold the toilet paper.

3   Using the crease as your guide, place a dot of glue on one half of the toilet paper, about an inch from the crease. Continue adding glue dots, spaced according to your seeds' needs. (See chapters 4 and 5 for spacing requirements.)

↑ Seed tapes are an easy and inexpensive DIY project during cold winter days. Pick out your favorite seeds, grab some toilet paper and glue, and you're ready to go!

SEED BOMBS

Have a guerilla gardener in your life? Can't stand passing that empty planter or unoccupied lot on the corner of your street? Need a gift for your favorite gardener? Seed bombs are a fun activity to keep your gardening hands busy. One word of advice before you dive in: think about a seed's needs. Many of the recipes posted online call for "handfuls" of seeds added to the mix. Too many seeds packed into a tiny space is wasteful—and a recipe for disaster. Overcrowded seedlings competing for water, nutrients, and airflow will weaken and eventually die. Use only a few seeds per bomb: two or three for seeds that germinate easily, four or five if germination is challenging.

Consider where you'd like the seed bombs to grow and choose varieties accordingly, based on climate, zone, sunlight needs, and possibly invasiveness issues. The best bet for seeds include easy annuals, like zinnias and cosmos, to brighten a sunny but barren space. If you're making a set as a gift, add a notecard that tells the recipient what seeds are included, as well as their preferred growing requirements.

INGREDIENTS

Note: *You'll be using clay and compost in a ratio of 1:1, so the quantity is your decision, depending on how many seed bombs you want to make. The quantity listed here makes a dozen seed bombs.*

- 1 cup aged compost, sifted
- 1 cup potter's clay
- 12" (30 cm) bowl
- Water
- Approximately 50 seeds
- Baking sheet

DIRECTIONS

1 In a bowl, moisten the clay by slowly adding water, mixing until the clay is the consistency of mashed potatoes.

2 Add the compost to the clay (maintaining the 1:1 ratio). Then add water to the compost and clay, mixing until it bonds but remains malleable.

3 Pinch off a tablespoon-sized segment of the mix and add a few seeds. Roll the mixture into a ball.

4 Place the balls on a baking sheet. Repeat the process until you've made all the seed bombs.

5 Place the baking sheet in a sunny location and allow the seed bombs to dry.

← Seed bombs are a fun craft to make with kids. They'll love getting messy, and you can sneak in a lesson about the environment too!

Winter Sowing

Winter sowing is one of the easiest ways to start seeds. All you need are recycled containers to serve as mini greenhouses, seed-starting mix, seeds, and Mother Nature!

Winter sowing mimics nature's seed starting but with an added boost. Using the mini greenhouses helps protect the seeds from wildlife, retains a bit of heat to the seeds for earlier germination, and provides natural stratification, which some seeds require for germination. In fact, for seeds that require stratification—the process of chilling seeds to encourage germination—you'll free up space in your refrigerator by winter sowing.

Additionally, winter sowing:

- Saves space by starting seeds outside.
- Saves money as no grow lights or heat mats are needed, nor do you incur the expense of electricity to power them.
- Saves time as there's no need to harden off seedlings prior to planting in the garden.

WINTER SOWING SUPPLIES

Supplies are minimal for winter sowing. Dig through your recycling bin or make a point to save the following items, which make perfect winter sowing containers:

- Plastic gallon-sized milk jugs
- Clear plastic 2-liter soda bottles
- Foil take-out containers with clear lids
- Aluminum cake pans with clear lids
- Any plastic container with a lid (you can cut out the top of opaque lids and replace with plastic wrap or insert the container in a clear zippered bag)

You'll also need:

- Sharp knife
- Packing tape
- Permanent marker or paint pen
- Plastic wrap or clear plastic bags
- Seeds
- Seed-starting mix
- Sunny space in the garden

↑ Upcycled containers are perfect for winter sowing.

How to Winter Sow Seeds

1 Select your containers. If you're using soda bottles or milk jugs, cut them in half around the middle, leaving a 1" (3 cm) segment attached to serve as a hinge to open the container on hot days. The hinge allows you to fold back the container's top for air circulation, while preventing its loss a on a windy day.

2 Cut drainage holes in the bottom of the containers.

3 Add 2–3" (5–8 cm) of seed-starting mix to the containers, then add seeds according to spacing requirements.

4 Cover the seeds with seed-starting mix, according to planting depth recommendations.

5 Water gently to settle the soil and seeds.

6 Place the clear cover (plastic wrap or plastic bags) onto the container. (If you're using milk jugs or soda bottles, reattach the top onto the bottom using clear packing tape.) Make sure the covers have holes to allow airflow and moisture to reach the seedlings.

7 Place the containers in a sunny location in the garden.

8 Check their progress weekly throughout winter, making sure the seed-starting mix stays moist.

9 As weather warms and seedlings emerge, remove the covers if there's no chance of frost. If it's a warm day, remove the cover so the seedlings don't overheat, but replace the cover again at night if frost threatens.

10 If temperatures are appropriate and seedlings have their first true leaves, transplant them into the garden. (Refer to chapters 4 and 5 for individual plant needs.)

CHAPTER 3

From Seedlings to Plants to Saving Seeds

You've successfully started your seeds, and your trays are filled with beautiful green seedlings. Congratulations! Now what? Much like anticipating the birth of a child, the more you prepare ahead of its arrival, the easier it will be to raise your little green babies.

Like any anxious new parent, you want only the best for your young. How can you make certain they're happy and healthy? How do you ensure they'll become productive members of society—wait, I mean, productive additions to your garden? In this chapter, we'll examine how to help your seedlings flourish into strong plants that will fill your garden with food and flowers. Then we'll continue the journey, harvesting, processing, and storing their seeds for next year's garden.

Care and Feeding of Seedlings

Your tiny seeds are now lovely little plants, crowding the trays with their first set of true leaves. How can you keep seedlings healthy until it's time to transplant? Just like newly germinated seeds, your seedlings still need:

Water: Check daily to ensure seed-starting mix is moist but not soggy. Don't allow seedlings to dry out. Fill the bottom of the tray with water and allow the plants' roots to wick it up to avoid disturbing seedlings. However, refrain from allowing plants to stand in water. If water remains in the tray after 12 hours, empty the excess.

↓ As seedheads dry in the garden, they add architectural interest to your landscape. Just make sure to harvest before the birds eat all your seeds.

Light: Continue to provide 12–16 hours of light for the seedlings. Make sure to raise the light fixture as the plants grow, keeping the light approximately 1 inch (3 cm) above the plants.

Airflow: Remove the humidity dome or plastic wrap after the seedlings emerge to promote good circulation.

Consistent temperature: Once the seedlings emerge, continue to monitor temperatures. Too cold, and you risk stunted plant growth. Too hot, and your seedlings might wilt and die.

Bully the Babies

It seems counterintuitive, but "roughing up" your seedlings will turn them into stronger plants. Now, I don't mean to mistreat them. After all, they are still fragile. However, brushing your hands over them several times a day will strengthen the stems, preparing them to withstand wind when they're planted in the garden. Some sources recommend an oscillating fan aimed at the seedlings. However, I find that trays dry out more quickly with a fan pointed at them, so I prefer the brushing technique.

TROUBLESHOOTING

Despite your best efforts when starting seeds, sometimes plans go awry and fate deals a cruel hand. What are the most common seed-starting challenges, and how you can combat them?

Failure to germinate: If you're not seeing any action, make sure your next planting starts with fresh, vigorous seeds. Test germination by placing a few seeds into a moistened, folded paper towel and enclose it in a plastic bag. Check every few days to see if the seeds sprout. If the seeds do not germinate, consider using new seeds. Also, follow the recommendations for seed starting in chapters 4 and 5, paying careful attention to challenging seeds that require stratification, scarification, or soaking. Use bottom heat for seeds that prefer it for germination.

Damping off: Nothing is more disheartening than watching your seeds germinate and begin to grow, only to find sudden seedling death. The culprit is most likely *damping off*, a fungal condition

that kills plants at the base of the stem. Once damping off occurs, there's nothing you can do to save the seedlings. However, you can avoid damping off by practicing good sanitization. Prior to planting, sterilize recycled containers in a solution of one-part bleach to nine-parts water, soaking the trays or containers to kill contaminants. Rinse containers with water after soaking. Use fresh seed-starting mix, not garden soil, which can harbor the fungus. Provide plenty of air circulation and avoid overwatering.

Discolored leaves or stems: Pale leaves or oddly colored seedling stems may indicate nutrient deficiency in a seedling. Use a good seed-starting mix that will support your plants until you transplant them. If you're delayed in potting up your seedlings and they're beginning to show stress, fertilize them with diluted fish emulsion or weak compost tea to provide a boost of nutrients. However, whitish leaves may indicate sunscald. Move the plants out of direct sunlight and back under grow lights until

they're properly acclimated to full, intense sunlight.

Leggy, weak seedlings: When seedlings stretch toward light, the plants suffer, forming weak stems. Place lights 1 inch above the plants, raising the lights as the plants grow. Make certain the seedlings receive 12–16 hours of light per day.

Mold: Too much watering is as bad as not enough. If the soil remains constantly wet, mold may develop on it. Water plants from the bottom and always check soil for moisture prior to watering.

Insects: Soil gnats don't cause damage but they are a nuisance in seedling trays—and they typically occur when soil is too wet. Other pests, like aphids, weaken plants and may spread diseases among your seedlings. Check seedlings for any sign of pests, particularly investigating the undersides of leaves. A yellow sticky trap inserted in trays can help reduce pest infestation. If the problem is severe, diluted Neem oil is a good organic solution to control pests on seedlings.

Into the Garden

Once the true leaves appear, it's time to kick your seedlings out of their current home and give them room to grow. What does that mean, exactly? Well, for seeds that you've grown indoors, it's time to pot up.

↑ By pampering your seedlings, they'll have strong, healthy roots, which will help them grow and produce well.

← Keep seedlings under lights and well watered so they grow into healthy transplants.

How to Pot Up Seedlings

- Prepare the containers and potting soil. If you plan to use recycled plant pots, make sure they've been sanitized. I use biodegradable containers, which can be planted straight into the garden.

- Fill the containers halfway with potting soil.

- Gently remove the seedlings from the tray. Use an old dinner fork to lift the seedling out of a propagation tray cell. If more than one seedling is growing per cell, separate the plants, gently teasing their roots apart.

- Insert the seedling into the container with potting soil. Add more soil to just below the first set of leaves.

- Firm the soil around the base of the plant's stem and adjust the plant to straighten it.

- Place the plants into a tray and move tray under grow lights.

- Water the plants thoroughly but don't overwater.

- Fertilize using diluted fish emulsion or compost tea once per week.

- Raise the grow lights as plants grow.

- Monitor water, light, and pests.

Potting Soil

Potting soil is my biggest expense when I grow seedlings. Because I grow for market, I'm not willing to take a chance on killing my precious, finicky plants by potting them up into garden soil that's potentially laden with fungus or bacteria that might kill them. I'm also too busy in spring to heat-treat garden soil to kill contaminants, plus heat treatment also kills good organisms in the soil. So, I buy many enormous bags of organic commercial potting soil.

However, as the plants grow and strengthen, I make sure the soil in the garden offers them the perfect environment to thrive. When creating new raised beds, I use the following soil formula to fill them, which is also a mix that can be used when potting up. It lessens the expense of buying multiple bags of pricey potting soil.

← Fill biodegradable pots partially with soil, then place the seedling and continue adding soil until its roots are covered and the plant is firmly situated in its new home.

COMBINE EQUAL PARTS:

- **Compost, aged and screened:** Make sure it's processed well and has reached the proper temperature to kill weed seeds and diseases. I like to blend well-rotted manure, leaf mold, and aged kitchen compost, making sure it's all screened very finely. (Remember, depending on temperature and components, a compost pile takes months to break down completely. Plan ahead.)
- **Bagged garden soil**
- **Vermiculite:** This is an important ingredient to improve soil aeration and retain water.

Mix the ingredients well in a container, ensuring equal distribution. Add water to moisten the soil, and you're ready to pot up! (When I'm preparing the mix for raised beds, I add the ingredients in layers in the bed, then mix them well with a rake or shovel to blend them.)

Prepping the Garden

Before you begin sowing seeds or planting transplants into your garden, take a survey of the area where you intend to plant. Much like a new home, it's easier to tackle renovations prior to moving into the garden.

Check your light: If you're planting food crops, you'll want an area with good sunlight, preferably 8 hours of full sun daily. Are there any limbs that need to be trimmed to provide more sun? Do you need to build a raised bed in a different location? The proper location is key for growing success, and it varies depending on your plants' needs.

Assess the soil: A soil test is the single best investment I recommend. Depending on what you plan to grow, a soil analysis tells you a soil's pH, the nutrients that are lacking (if any), as well as how to balance the soil so your plants will thrive. Soil test kits are available online and at garden centers. However, many university cooperative extension programs offer soil testing for a small fee. For the price of a cup of

fancy coffee, you can receive a full report on your soil that tells how you need to amend it to grow your favorite plants.

Remove any weeds from the beds: Weeds compete with your seedlings, siphoning off water and nutrients. Clean the beds prior to planting.

Clear a flat spot in the garden to harden off seedlings: You'll be transitioning seedlings from shade to partial sun to full sun for about two weeks. Make sure you have access to a water source, both near the seedlings and in the garden for the beds.

Clean and repair your tools: Sterilize clippers and trowels to ensure you don't pass along any diseases. Also repair leaky hoses or irrigation systems. Replace any broken boards for raised beds or damaged plant supports in the garden as well. (I also use an alcohol wipe to sterilize nonporous supports.)

Remove leaves and debris: If you didn't clean up the garden beds in the fall, it's time, particularly if you're growing food crops. Remove hiding places that shelter voles or pest insects. Also remove any rocks that impede planting.

Add screened compost: After checking my soil, I almost always add finished, screened compost to my raised beds. Rake it in well, breaking up any soil clumps, and smooth the bed.

As your plants grow and thrive in your garden, continue to monitor them for water and pest issues. Add an organic fertilizer if needed for plants that are heavy feeders, like tomatoes. Some plants require staking as they grow.

Remember: the more time you spend in the garden, the more likely you'll catch problems early, which can save your harvest. Make a habit of walking through the garden daily, both for pleasure and to check your plants' progress.

WHY AND HOW TO HARDEN OFF SEEDLINGS

Spring is close, and you're anxious to start your garden. The last projected frost date is near—hooray! Time to plant . . . or is it?

Before you take your trays to the garden to plant those precious green babies you've nurtured for months, you need to gently introduce them to their new environment. After all, those tender plants aren't accustomed to bright sunlight, wind, or chilly evenings. Spend a few weeks preparing the transplants for their new home so they will thrive.

First, find a level spot in your garden that's protected from wind. Place your trays there for an hour to begin introducing the plants to the great outdoors, extending their outside time by an hour each day. If the area is partially sunny, perfect. After a few days, allow the plants more sunlight. Move the plants so they receive an hour or two of full sun for few days, increasing the exposure a bit each day. Be careful to avoid sunscald—take it slowly. If the weather is cold, move the trays inside at night.

Monitor the plants' water needs. Plants will be thirsty in this new environment of wind and sun. Don't let them dry out. Conversely, if they've withstood a rainstorm, make certain to pour standing water out of the trays.

Continue exposing the plants to more sun each day, until they're finally in full sun for 6–8 hours. If the conditions are right—temperatures are appropriate for the crops you're planting and the danger of frost has passed for tender plants—you can now transition the plants into their final garden home.

Ensuring Pure Seeds

As a slightly obsessive seed lover, I've been known to fill my pockets with seeds from my garden, from friends' gardens, and from nature outings. (Don't collect seeds from botanical gardens without permission though. The staff horticulturist may have plans for those seeds.)

Random seed collecting is fun but not exacting. If you're looking to maintain varietal purity, it's important to plan ahead in your garden and follow fairly simple techniques to ensure the seeds you collect are true to the parent plant. After all, if you've fallen in love with 'Chinese 5-Color' peppers, you'll want to ensure that the seeds you save from them are indeed 'Chinese 5-Color' peppers, not a new hybrid created by rogue pollen introduced by a busy bee. (Remember: save seeds from open-pollinated plants, not hybrids, as discussed in chapter 1.)

Note that the seed-saving techniques I'm sharing in this book are intended for the home gardener. Commercial seed production occurs on a much larger scale and with much greater acreage than most home gardeners possess. Also, commercial seed production must include many, many factors, such as promoting genetic diversity, increasing population size, eliminating plants with undesirable characteristics . . . all things that help perpetuate the specific plant varieties and ensure their future availability. While these factors are important and home gardeners need to adopt some of the ideas, saving seeds in the home garden doesn't need to be as complicated as producing seeds for commercial sale.

Remember: You don't need to worry about cross-pollination with some plants, but with others it's important to avoid cross-pollination. For each plant entry in chapters 4 and 5, you'll find specific seed-saving preparation and techniques listed in the details. The primary methods include isolation distance and timing, bagging, and caging. Also, remember that you'll need to plant several—even a dozen or more—of the same variety to maintain genetic diversity and avoid inbreeding depression.

↑ It's important to avoid cross-pollination when saving seeds, or you might experience an unpleasant surprise in next year's garden due to impure seeds.

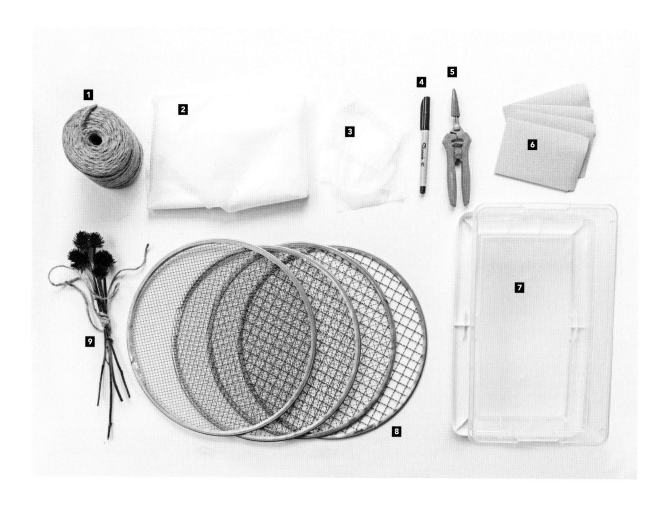

↑ Seed-saving supplies,
clockwise from left:

1 twine
2 row cover cloth
3 blossom bag
4 marker
5 snips
6 envelopes
7 storage container
8 seed cleaning screens
9 *Echinacea* seedheads

WHAT IS INBREEDING DEPRESSION?

It's important to grow many of the same varieties of plants to avoid inbreeding depression. If you're unfamiliar with this term, inbreeding depression is the loss of vigor within a population due to breeding genetically similar plants. In commercial production, growers plant dozens or hundreds of the same plant to use for pollination and, ultimately, seed production. In the home garden, it's less important for an immense population size than those seeds grown for commercial distribution or inclusion in seed banks (and, honestly, it's challenging due to space constraints). However, it is important to harvest seeds from several plants to avoid disappointment in future crops. Planting many of the same variety also gives you options when selecting which plants are best for seed saving. If ten zinnias are covered in powdery mildew but twenty are disease free, you'll have plenty of clean plants from which to save seeds.

Distance and Time Isolation

Isolation refers to the practice of growing crops away from any other variety that might lead to cross-pollination. There are three main ways to isolate plants and *distance isolation* is the most challenging for home gardeners.

There are several reasons for this. To start, most distance isolation recommendations range from 800 feet to several miles, a bit much for most home gardeners. While barriers, like a tall hedge or wall surrounding the garden, can lessen the distance isolation requirements, structural barriers don't provide absolute isolation to ensure pure seeds. Also, unless you form an arrangement with your neighbors to grow only the same varieties that are in your garden, you risk cross-pollination. Even if you have the space, insects and wind are also a factor. It's nearly impossible to control the insects that visit your garden. Bees travel miles and wind is unpredictable, reaching through cracks and across distances to cross-pollinate wind-pollinated plants.

Time isolation is better for home gardeners but still a bit cumbersome. The method is just what it sounds like: If you have crops that you'd like to grow together but that may cross-pollinate, like lettuce, simply select ones with different bloom times. Check the maturity dates of the crops before you begin and plan accordingly. Plant the earliest-maturing crop first. As it flowers, sow seeds for the second variety. The first variety should set its seeds prior to the second crop beginning to flower, avoiding cross-pollination. (If any flowers remain on the first crop after seed setting, pinch off the blooms before the second crop can flower.)

Mechanical Isolation Such as Bagging and Caging

Now we come to the third option, *mechanical isolation*. In this case I've saved the best for last as mechanical isolation is the technique I recommend for most home gardeners. It relies on two simple techniques: bagging and caging.

Bagging refers to placing a bag or cloth over a plant's flowers to prevent cross-pollination by insects or wind. (Even self-pollinating plants risk cross-pollination from insects.) While you can bag an entire plant, it's inconvenient for tall plants and simpler to focus on the flowers. Bags are constructed from lightweight, light-colored fabric, like spun polyester cloth or tulle. Small organza gift bags found in dollar stores make perfect blossom bags. If the bag doesn't have a drawstring, a twist tie works well to secure it tightly to a plant's stem. Do not, however, use clear plastic bags, as they lack proper ventilation and may cause the plants to overheat in direct sun. Bagging is best for self-pollinated plants, but you can also hand-pollinate the flowers that typically require assistance of insects or wind. Here's how:

1 Start by placing the bag over the plant's flower bud before it begins to open. Secure the bag tightly around the stem so that insects can't enter. If you're bagging a cluster of flowers and one has already opened, pinch off that bloom to avoid any potential of prior cross-contamination.

2 If the plant is not self-fertile, remove the bag briefly when the flowers open and hand-pollinate the blooms. Do not allow insects onto the flowers. Replace the bag immediately.

3 Leave the bag in place until the plant forms an immature fruit or seed. Remove the bag, as no chance of cross-pollination remains.

4 Mark the fruit or seedpod with a ribbon or tape to indicate that it's to harvest for seed saving upon maturity.

5 Allow the fruit to grow unimpeded.

While bagging is a good option for many plants, it doesn't protect all plants, particularly those with extremely fine-grained pollen. Check the notes in chapters 4 and 5 to determine which plants benefit from bagging.

Caging is similar to bagging but on a larger scale. While both techniques protect plants from cross-pollination, bagging focuses on individual or smaller clusters of blooms for seed saving, while caging can protect an entire plant or even groups of the same variety of plants. Several options work well for caging:

- Use the same lightweight fabric, like row cover cloth or tulle, to cover the entire plant, securing it at the base of the plant.

- Cover a tomato cage with the fabric, securing the fabric to the cage and also to the base of the plant.

- Build a cage out of wood and staple a fine-mesh screen or row cover fabric to cover the frame. Constructing a cage allows you to customize it to accommodate your garden's specific size needs.

While the cage keeps out unwanted pollen, it also bans pollinators. For crops that require the assistance of pollinators to produce fruit, you have two options: introduce pollinators into cages or hand-pollinate plants.

→ Bagging blooms to prevent cross-pollination is one of the easiest ways for home gardeners to ensure pure seeds.

Introducing pollinators to your cage can be a bit tricky. Attracting bees to a plate of honey is the easy part. Moving them into the caged setting isn't too challenging. (If you're allergic to bees, enlist someone to handle this step for you.) The bees will initially attempt to escape the cage, but eventually they should settle in and begin enjoying the blooms. Once immature fruit or seeds form on the plants, release the bees.

For many gardeners, myself included, hand-pollinating caged plants presents a better option. Hand-pollination involves collecting pollen from male flowers and transferring it onto stigmas of female flowers to produce fruit and seeds that remain true to type. An inexpensive artist's paintbrush is a perfect tool to pollinate many plants, but hand-pollination techniques vary by plant. Check chapters 4 and 5 for specific plant requirements. Remember: make certain to replace the cage or bag after hand-pollinating, leaving it in place until fruit or seeds develop. You don't want some sneaky bee or butterfly ruining your work!

- -

WHAT IS VERNALIZATION?

Some plants, like cabbage and carrots, only produce flowers (and seeds) after a period of chilling. For many biennials and perennials, the plants remain in their vegetative state through the warm season, chill in winter, then continue to grow in the spring, eventually bearing flowers and fruit.

While the process takes place easily in nature, we've learned to trick plants into flowering through vernalization, which is an artificially induced chilling period that shortens the vegetative phase, speeds flowering, and, ultimately, seed production. Stay tuned for more details in chapter 4 about plants that require vernalization to produce seeds, as well as how to chill those plants.

↑ Many plants need pollinators in order to produce seeds. Introduce pollinators into cages so pollinators can reach blooms. If that's not an option, you can hand-pollinate flowers.

Harvesting and Processing Seeds

One of the most important aspects of seed saving is to consider your plants when harvesting. Is your pepper productive or slow to produce fruit? Does your bean plant thrive, or is it covered in powdery mildew? Are you constantly battling aphids on tomato plants, or are you eating fruit straight off the vine, free of pests?

Select desirable plants by observing your plants throughout the season, instead of just judging the fruit. Selecting healthy, productive, drought-tolerant, and disease-resistant plants provides seeds with similar characteristics. That said, you should also consider the color, shape, size, productivity, and flavor of the fruit, as those are the fruits or flowers you want to replicate in your garden next year. You can even judge the seeds: bigger is better. Save the largest seeds from your harvest, as they'll generally produce the most vigorous plants.

When harvesting your fruits and seeds, you'll also need to make certain you're confident of the variety. I know it seems like you'll never forget what's planted where when you set out those precious little seedlings in the spring. However, life happens. Memories fade, plant tags disappear. As soon as I plant my garden, I take a photo of each bed and then I write down (in order by row) the varieties that are planted there. Is it a little obsessive? Yes. But my obsessive recording has also saved my sanity on more than one occasion.

Last but not least, you'll need to harvest when the fruits or vegetables are mature. For some plants, like tomatoes, the seeds ripen at the same time as the fruit, making harvests simple. Eat the fruit, save the seeds. For others, like fennel, seeds need to dry on the plant or remain within an overripe fruit, like eggplant, to achieve maturity. Sometimes, seeds on one plant, such as the umbel of dill, don't ripen all at once. You'll find information on when to harvest each variety in chapters 4 and 5.

← Be careful! Some seedheads, such as those from chives and leeks, shatter easily, scattering seeds into the garden if they're not harvested gently.

Wet Processing

You've harvested the fruit and flower seedheads from the garden. Now, how do you save the seeds? Most seeds fall into two processing categories: wet processing and dry processing.

Wet processing is used to remove seeds embedded in the wet flesh of fruit. Melons, tomatoes, and cucumbers, for instance, fall into wet processing seed collection. Wet processing is a bit more involved than dry processing, but it's still quite simple.

Remove the seed from the fruit. This might involve squeezing tomato seeds and the pulp into a container or grating eggplant to remove the seeds from the flesh. Sometimes the seeds need to go through a fermentation process. (Specific cleaning techniques for each plant are listed in chapters 4 and 5.) Ferment the seed mix, if needed (see page 52).

Wash the seeds. To clean seeds and separate them from pulp or fermentation mixture, add twice the amount of water as the volume of seeds and pulp. Stir vigorously to clean. Allow the mixture to settle. Nonviable, hollow seeds and pulp/debris will float to the top of the mix.

Take a strainer and scoop off this top layer. The viable seeds will sink to the bottom of the container. Add more water, stir to clean the seeds one more time, then pour the water through a fine-mesh strainer, collecting the seeds. Using a paper towel, blot the bottom of the strainer to absorb excess water.

Dry the seeds. Pour seeds onto a nonstick surface, like a plate, to dry. (Do not place seeds on a paper towel as they will stick to it when drying.) Spread seeds into a single layer, shaking the plate gently each day to ensure even drying. Protect seeds from excessively high temperatures. Never dry seeds in an oven or in direct sunlight.

↑ When seeds are embedded into the fruit's flesh, like with eggplant, use a grater as the first step in separating the seeds.

↑ Add water to the seeds and pulp and allow the mixture to separate. Pulp and debris will rise to the top, where you can skim it off. Viable seeds settle to the bottom.

↑ After separating the seeds from the pulp, rinse them well.

← Allow the mix to settle. The pulp and nonviable seeds will rise to the top, where they can be skimmed off with a fine-mesh strainer.

THE IMPORTANCE OF FERMENTATION

Fermentation occurs naturally in a garden. When a fruit falls to the ground, it ferments and rots, breaking down the protective gel coating surrounding a seed that keeps it from germinating. Think about the volunteer tomato plants you find in the garden. They've undergone nature's version of fermentation.

When seed saving, we mimic nature's handiwork. The fermentation process is important to seed saving, as the microorganisms it produces destroy many seed-borne diseases that affect future plants.

Fermentation time may be influenced by temperature, as well as too much water added to the seed mix. (I add only a small amount of water to seed mix if there's not much moisture present.) Also, watch the mix carefully. Once a layer of mold appears on the surface of the seed mix, it's time to clean the seeds. Don't wait too long, as the seeds may begin to germinate.

Wash the seeds, rinsing them through a strainer, to clean them. For a step-by-step description of fermenting tomato seeds, see chapter 4.

Dry Processing

Dry processing occurs when seeds are harvested from pods or husks that dried on the plant. Beans, peas, okra, brassicas, lettuce, radish, carrot umbels, and corn, to name a few, fall under dry processing.

Dry processing is simple: Collect the seedheads and seedpods when they're fully dried and clean accordingly. If a freeze threatens before the seeds have matured and dried on the plant, you can harvest the entire plant, hang it in a shed or garage that doesn't freeze, and allow the seeds to continue to mature on the plant. Harvest the pods as they dry.

Some plants are rather stubborn about releasing their seeds. Other plants encase the seeds in quite a bit of fluff, and there's much debris when harvesting. Yet separating seeds is generally easy if you know how.

Threshing involves breaking seeds free from their coverings. While some seeds come free easily with a vigorous shake or by rubbing the seedheads with your fingers, others are quite prickly. Threshing includes rubbing, beating, and flailing seedpods to release seeds. An old pillowcase is a perfect tool. Place any stubborn seedpods inside the pillowcase and jump on it to break open the pods. Or close one end of the pillowcase with a rubber band and whack it over a rock. Pummeling the pillowcase with a rolling pin is also quite effective in releasing seeds, plus it's therapeutic if you're having a bad day.

Placing seedpods between two boards and mashing the pods also works well to separate seeds. However, only use this technique for small seeds. You may accidentally split larger seeds, like beans, with the boards.

↑ Some seedheads, such as those from artichokes, require winnowing to separate the seeds from chaff.

↑ Bean seeds are some of the easiest to save. Allow the pods to dry on the vine until they're brown, then simply open the pods and remove the seeds.

Once you've released the seeds, it's time to winnow. *Winnowing* is the process of separating the debris and chaff from the seeds. If you're only saving a small amount of seeds, winnowing is easily accomplished by hand. However, for larger quantities, a small fan or hair dryer set on the coolest setting helps separate chaff from seeds. Make sure to cover your work space with cloth or plastic. Collect the seeds, and then shake out the drop cloth to remove debris. Make certain the cloth is clean before you begin cleaning the next variety to ensure seeds remain separate.

If you're saving a large quantity of seeds, you may want to build a seed-screening station. A graduated series of screens allows chaff to remain in the top layer, while smaller debris falls through to the bottom screen, with the seeds caught in the middle screen, depending on seed size.

Use several sizes of mesh screen: fine, medium, and coarse. Stack the screens so that the mesh with the largest opening is on top, the medium-sized mesh is in the middle, and the finest mesh is on the bottom. Pour the seeds on top of the screens and shake them, helping the seeds to separate from the chaff. Remove the clean seeds from the screen to store and clean the debris from the screens.

Storing and Preserving Seeds

Once you've cleaned your seeds, it's time to store them for your future garden. You've worked hard, growing beautiful plants, enjoying their fruit, and harvesting their seeds. You've tolerated the stench of fermentation, pricked your fingers harvesting okra pods, and chased milkweed fluff throughout your house. Your friends teased you about the dozens of paper plates residing on the dining room table, carefully marked with variety names and filled with drying seeds. Well done, you!

Now stay vigilant for one more step, so that you're not undoing all your efforts: Store your seeds carefully. It's not difficult, I promise, particularly with seeds harvested from a typical kitchen garden or cutting bed. Simply remember these three words: cool, dry, and dark.

Most seeds are resilient, but keep in mind that each seed is alive. While a seed wants nothing more than to perpetuate, bringing new life into the world, protect it so that it remains viable. By removing environmental factors that damage seeds, like moisture, direct sunlight, and fluctuating temperatures, you're slowing a seed's metabolism without damaging the embryo within the seed coat. Store seeds in a cool location, out of direct sunlight (preferably in the dark), and away from dampness. Easy, right? After all, most of us can sacrifice space on a bedroom closet shelf to store our precious seeds.

Stored in proper conditions, many seeds remain viable for years. However, viability varies per plant. Refer to chapters 4 and 5 to gauge how long your seeds may last. (In a cruel twist of fate, some weed seeds can remain viable for half a century, much longer than most of the crops gardeners hope to grow! It's not fair, I know.)

Package seeds in small paper envelopes, carefully labeled with the date harvested and varietal name. Make certain the seeds dry completely before storage because moisture threatens seed viability. No one wants to open carefully collected packages of seeds to find a disappointing, moldy mess.

For an added layer of security, place the envelopes into an air-tight canning jar or container. Store the container in a cool, dry, dark location. Then you can rest. You've successfully completed the journey of gardening from seed to seed! Congratulations!

Now, it's time to start dreaming of next year's garden . . .

MEET
THE PLANTS

CHAPTER 4

Fruits and Vegetables

Is there anything more satisfying than preparing dinner using vegetables from your garden that you started from seed? It's a fabulous feeling to know that you started plants, nurtured them, harvested their fruit, and saved seed from those plants for next year's garden. You've become a fully self-sufficient gardener!

The first three chapters of this book provided the information you need to get started on your seed-starting and -saving journey. Now, let's dive into the specific plants and their needs so you'll grow an amazing, productive garden. The plants here are organized alphabetically by their Latin names.

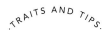

COMMON NAME: Okra

SCIENTIFIC NAME: *Abelmoschus esculentus*

FAMILY: Malvaceae, same family as cotton and mallow

LIFE CYCLE: Annual

FRUIT TYPE: Capsule

SEED-STARTING DEPTH: ½" (1.3 cm)

SPECIAL NEEDS: Scarification or soak seeds for 12 hours in warm water prior to planting.

SEED-STARTING SOIL TEMPERATURE: 70–95°F (21–35°C)

SEED START TIMING: Direct sow after frost is preferred. Can be started indoors using biodegradable containers 4–5 weeks before last frost. Bottom heat speeds germination.

LIGHT REQUIREMENTS: As soon as seedlings emerge

TRANSPLANT: After danger of frost. Do not disturb roots. Plant in deep beds, as okra grows a long taproot. Space 18" (46 cm) apart for smaller varieties, 36" (91 cm) apart for tall varieties.

DIRECT SOWING: After danger of frost and when temperatures reach 55°F (13°C)

GERMINATION: 3–12 days

DAYS TO MATURITY: 50–60

POLLINATION: Self

CROSS-POLLINATION: Can cross-pollinate with other okra varieties. Cage plants or bag blossoms to prevent cross-pollination.

ISOLATION DISTANCE: ½ mile (0.8 km)

SEED MATURITY: Dry pods on the plants or harvest prior to frost and allow pods to continue to dry fully. Wear gloves to harvest pods.

SEED PROCESSING: Thresh to remove seeds from pods.

SEED VIABILITY: 2–3 years

Okra
Abelmoschus esculentus

It's a love/hate relationship with okra. My Southern friends consider it a necessary garden staple, adding it to gumbo or frying it, while other people can't abide its somewhat slimy nature. Still, with its beautiful blooms, okra deserves a place in your garden. Most okra varieties are daylight sensitive, flowering early with shorter days. Okra produces perfect flowers that are self-pollinating. However, pollinators adore their large, showy flowers, so cross-pollination is possible. Bag the blooms to avoid cross-pollination. Edible pods form 5 to 7 days after the blossom appears. Harvest the pods to eat while they're young, as they become woody as they age.

Leek
Allium ampeloprasum

I'll admit my Swiss husband introduced me to leeks, because it seems they're more popular in Europe than in the United States. Now, not only do I use them at least twice weekly, I grow them too. After all, leeks can be a bit pricey at the supermarket, and they're incredibly easy to grow. Plus, as an allium, leeks produce beautiful blooms, which the pollinators adore.

Leeks require patience, with a long growing season of approximately 120 days. They prefer deep, humus-rich beds with steady moisture. The good news is that leeks tolerate mild winters well. In fact, you can plant a fall crop in Southern climates to harvest leeks in the winter. However, in cold climates, leeks need to be dug and stored to protect them, then replanted in the spring. Although leeks are classified as biennials, they may produce flower stalks the first year, after 4 to 6 weeks of cold temperatures. However, the plant needs to grow to maturity the second year before harvesting seed, as the seed will not be viable.

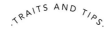

LEEK

COMMON NAME: Leek

SCIENTIFIC NAME: *Allium ampeloprasum*

FAMILY: Amaryllidaceae

LIFE CYCLE: Biennial

FRUIT TYPE: Capsule

SEED-STARTING DEPTH: ¼" (0.6 cm)

SPECIAL NEEDS: Requires vernalization period, with temperatures below 55°F (13°C) for 4–6 weeks to induce flowering and seed setting.

SEED-STARTING SOIL TEMPERATURE: 50–75°F (10–24°C)

SEED START TIMING: Direct sowing after frost is preferred. Can be started indoors using biodegradable containers 4–5 weeks before last frost. Can also be planted in fall in mild climates.

LIGHT REQUIREMENTS: As soon as seedlings emerge

TRANSPLANT: Plant after danger of frost. Plant in a 6" (15 cm) deep trench, 2" (5 cm) apart. Fill in sides with soil as plants grow.

DIRECT SOWING: Sow after danger of frost has passed and when temperatures reach 55°F (13°C).

GERMINATION: 5–7 days

DAYS TO MATURITY: 80–120

POLLINATION: Self

CROSS-POLLINATION: Can cross-pollinate with other varieties. Cage plants or bag blossoms to prevent cross-pollination.

ISOLATION DISTANCE: ½ mile (0.8 km)

SEED MATURITY: Allow flower heads (capsules) to dry on plants. Harvest when capsules fade or begin to split, showing dark seeds within.

SEED PROCESSING: Thresh

SEED VIABILITY: 2–3 years

Celery and Celeriac
Apium graveolens var. *dulce* (celery), *Apium graveolens* var. *rapaceum* (celeriac)

Although they share a similar flavor, celery and celeriac grow differently and serve different culinary functions. Celery, with its tall stems and flat leaves, is 94 percent water, adding crunch and texture to dishes. Celeriac, with its dense, bulbous, yellowish root, provides a great addition to soups, stews, and gratins. Both celery and celeriac are biennial plants requiring pollination from insects, and both require a chilling period to flower and produce seed. In mild climates, overwinter the plants in the ground and insulate with a layer of mulch, but in cold zones, dig up the roots and store in a root cellar. Trim celery stalks severely and place the roots in damp earth or sand with crowns exposed. For celeriac, carefully dig the bulbous root, trim the roots and top, and store in a container filled with damp sand at 33–40°F (0.5–4°C). When weather warms, remove any dead vegetation and replant the celery and celeriac in the garden.

CELERY AND CELERIAC

COMMON NAMES: Celery, celeriac

SCIENTIFIC NAMES: *Apium graveolens* var. *dulce, Apium graveolens* var. *rapaceum*

FAMILY: Apiaceae

LIFE CYCLE: Biennial

FRUIT TYPE: Umbel

SEED-STARTING DEPTH: ¼" (0.6 cm)

SPECIAL NEEDS: Soak seeds overnight to speed germination. It needs light to germinate.

SEED-STARTING SOIL TEMPERATURE: 55–75°F (13–24°C). Seeds sown in temperatures exceeding 85°F (29°C) remain dormant.

SEED START TIMING: Direct sow when soil temperature reaches 50°F (10°C). Start seeds for transplants 10–12 weeks before last expected frost date. Can also be grown in mild climates for a fall crop.

LIGHT REQUIREMENTS: It needs light to germinate. As seedlings emerge, continue 12–16 hours of light per day.

TRANSPLANT: Plant after danger of frost. Space plants 10–12" (25–30 cm) for celery, 6–8" (15–20 cm) for celeriac. Both like compost-rich, moist soil. Celery prefers a pH of 5.8–6.8. Celeriac is a heavy feeder. Water weekly with compost tea.

DIRECT SOWING: After danger of frost

GERMINATION: 14–21 days

DAYS TO MATURITY: 100–130 celery; 90–120 celeriac

POLLINATION: Insect

CROSS-POLLINATION: Can cross-pollinate with other varieties. Cage plants or bag blossoms to prevent cross-pollination. Hand-pollinate or introduce pollinators into cage.

ISOLATION DISTANCE: 1 mile (1.6 km)

SEED MATURITY: Seeds mature the second year. If seeds are produced the first year, they will not be viable. Harvest seeds when color turns from green to brown.

SEED PROCESSING: Screen

SEED VIABILITY: 3–6 years

Asparagus
Asparagus officinalis

Growing asparagus is an exercise in patience, which is not my forté. It's hard to resist those delicious shoots peeking out of the soil in the spring. But eating the first spear straight from the garden makes the wait worthwhile. And you will wait—three years, to be exact—before harvesting your first, precious asparagus. While growing asparagus from seed is easy, it takes several years to establish a strong, productive plant.

Before you transplant seedlings into the garden, remember: Asparagus is a perennial. Select your location carefully as the bed will become its permanent home. Choose a site that drains well and amend it with compost. Asparagus prefers a soil pH between 6.5 and 7.0. Based on the results of a soil test, determine if you need to add lime to the bed to raise the pH. If the pH is too high, amend the soil with sulfur. (Test your soil early, as it can take several months to establish the correct soil pH.) Allow the plants to grow for two years, with the spears becoming ferns and then dying back each season. Finally, in year three, you may begin harvesting a few spears in the spring.

The trick to saving seeds is to know the difference between male and female asparagus plants. Male varieties, while typically providing larger spears, don't produce fruit, which means that only female asparagus plants produce seeds. To clean the seeds, crush the berries in a bag, then soak them in a bowl of water. Debris and nonviable seeds will rise to the top. Remove the debris, then pour the remaining water and seeds through a fine sieve. Dry the seeds on a plate for a week. **NOTE:** The bright red asparagus berries are toxic. Do not eat them.

ASPARAGUS

COMMON NAME: Asparagus

SCIENTIFIC NAME: *Asparagus officinalis*

FAMILY: Liliaceae

LIFE CYCLE: Perennial

FRUIT TYPE: Berry

SEED-STARTING DEPTH: ½" (1.3 cm)

SPECIAL NEEDS: Soak seeds overnight prior to planting.

SEED-STARTING SOIL TEMPERATURE: 70–80°F (21–27°C)

SEED START TIMING: Indoors 8–10 weeks before first frost

LIGHT REQUIREMENTS: As soon as seedlings emerge

TRANSPLANT: Plant after danger of frost. Do not disturb roots. Plant in deep beds, as asparagus grows large roots. Space plants 15" (38 cm) apart, with 36" (91 cm) between rows. Avoid transplanting after the second year.

DIRECT SOWING: Sow after danger of frost has passed and when soil temperatures reach 70°F (21°C).

GERMINATION: 7–21 days

DAYS TO MATURITY: 3 years until the first harvest

POLLINATION: Insect

CROSS-POLLINATION: Can cross-pollinate with wild asparagus. Cage plants or bag blossoms to prevent cross-pollination.

ISOLATION DISTANCE: ¼ mile (0.4 km)

SEED MATURITY: Let berries dry on plants, or harvest prior to frost and dry.

SEED PROCESSING: Wet processing

SEED VIABILITY: 3 years

↑ Swiss chard

Beets and Swiss Chard
Beta vulgaris (Crassa group),
Beta vulgaris (Cicla group)

Beet seeds are finicky, as their seed coat contains a chemical that inhibits germination. Luckily an overnight soaking in water remedies the problem. Did you know that the seed is actually a cluster of multiple seeds? So don't fret over careful spacing when sowing seeds, as you'll still need to thin plants. (Benefit: baby beet and swiss chard seedlings make a tasty addition to salads.)

Both beets and swiss chard require a chill period before producing seeds the second year. In mild climates, cut the tops, dig the roots to inspect them for quality, and replant the healthiest, largest, disease-free beets, adding a layer of mulch to protect the plant. For swiss chard, harvest the leaves, cutting them to an inch above the roots, and leave in the ground. Cover with mulch.

However, in cold climates, both crops must be dug and stored away from freezing temperatures. Store in a root cellar or basement at 40°F (4°C). Replant in the spring when danger of freezing temperatures has passed.

BEETS AND SWISS CHARD

COMMON NAMES: Beet, swiss chard

SCIENTIFIC NAMES: *Beta vulgaris* (beet: Crassa group); *Beta vulgaris* (swiss chard: Cicla group)

FAMILY: Amaranthacea (formerly Chenopodiaceae)

LIFE CYCLE: Biennial

FRUIT TYPE: Dry, indehiscent fruit, multigerm (seedball)

SEED-STARTING DEPTH: ½" (1.3 cm)

SPECIAL NEEDS: Soak seeds overnight prior to planting.

SEED-STARTING SOIL TEMPERATURE: Optimal is 85°F (29°C); can germinate at 45°F (7°C)

SEED START TIMING: Direct sowing is preferred. Can be started indoors and planted in the garden 1–2 weeks before last frost.

LIGHT REQUIREMENTS: As soon as seedlings emerge

TRANSPLANT: Plant 1–2 weeks prior to last frost. Space 8–10" (20–25 cm) in rows 12–24" (30–61 cm) apart.

DIRECT SOWING: Sow when temperatures reach 45°F (7°C) minimum. Protect young plants from freezing.

GERMINATION: 5–16 days

DAYS TO MATURITY: 55–80 beet; 50–60 swiss chard

POLLINATION: Wind. Plants, with perfect, self-incompatible flowers, require outward pollination. Self-incompatible plants, while producing functional pollen, fail to set seeds when self-pollinated and need pollen from another plant to reproduce.

CROSS-POLLINATION: Swiss chard and beets may cross. Cage the same types of plants in groups with extremely fine covering to avoid cross-pollination by wind.

ISOLATION DISTANCE: 800'–1 mile (0.24–1.6 km)

SEED MATURITY: Requires vernalization. Seeds ripen first at the base of side shoots, then progress to terminal points. Color changes from green to brown, but harvest time is challenging to identify; cut open a sample seed to gauge maturity. Unripe seed is milky; ripe is mealy.

SEED PROCESSING: Thresh

SEED VIABILITY: 5 years

↑ Beets

Brassicas

Brassica juncea (mustards)

Brassica napus (rutabaga, Siberian Kale, Swede)

Brassica oleracae (brussels sprouts, broccoli, cabbage, cauliflower, Chinese broccoli, collards, kale, kohlrabi, sprouting broccoli)

Brassica rapa (broccoli raab, Chinese cabbage, Napa cabbage, turnip)

Ah, brassicas . . . the stars of the cool-season garden. While it might seem odd to group all brassicas together, there is a method to my madness. Most brassicas share common seed-starting traits, and many grow under the same garden conditions. However, when varieties deviate from the pack, you'll find those specific needs defined.

Most brassicas thrive under full sun or partial shade (but need at least 4–5 hours of sun). Brassicas prefer a soil pH between 6–7, and they appreciate well-drained, compost-rich soil. While brassicas that grow quickly often taste the best, those that require a longer growing season benefit from additional fertilizer. Compost tea or diluted fish emulsion will boost plant growth. The biggest challenge is timing: brassicas grow best in cool weather and bolt in summer's heat. In fact, most brassicas taste sweeter after they've been kissed by frost.

↑ Kohlrabi

↑ Broccoli

↑ Brussels sprouts

↑ Brassica blooms need pollination for seed production, but bag the flowers to avoid cross-pollination.

Watch for pests, particularly cabbage worms and loopers. I remove them by hand (they become chicken treats) but look carefully for eggs on the undersides of leaves, which you can simply squish. One of the best methods to prevent pest damage is to place a floating row cover over brassica crops after planting seedlings. The lightweight cover protects them from cabbage moths, which lay the eggs, plus it's easily removed to weed or water the plants.

Brassicas require that pesky vernalization period before you can harvest seed. In my Southern garden, I leave fall-planted brassicas in the ground, mulching well around the plants, and let nature take its course. In cold climates, it's still best to select fall-planted brassicas to overwinter indoors, as the plants are smaller and require less storage space than brassicas that grew all summer. For root crops, dig the root, remove foliage, and store in damp growing medium in a cool, dark place, like a basement or root cellar. For crops like cabbage or kale, harvest exterior leaves, keep the growing point intact (the flower stalk will form here), check carefully for pests, and pot up into containers. Store in a basement or root cellar. As spring approaches, inspect the plants for signs of rot or root damage, remove dead foliage, and replant in the garden a month prior to the last expected frost date. Space plants approximately 18–24 inches (46–61 cm) in rows spaced 36 inches (91 cm) apart.

Allow the plants to continue to grow and form flower stalks. Brassicas are insect-pollinated. Cage plants and introduce pollinators as needed.

BRASSICAS

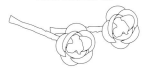

COMMON NAMES/SCIENTIFIC NAMES:

• Mustard/*Brassica juncea*

• Rutabaga, Siberian kale, Swede/*Brassica napus*

• Brussels sprouts, broccoli, cabbage, cauliflower, Chinese broccoli, collards, kale, kohlrabi, sprouting broccoli/*Brassica oleracae*

• Broccoli raab, Chinese cabbage, Napa cabbage, turnip/*Brassica rapa*

FAMILY: Brassicaceae

LIFE CYCLE: Biennial

FRUIT TYPE: Solique

SEED-STARTING DEPTH: ¼" (0.6 cm)

SPECIAL NEEDS: If seedborne disease is an issue in your garden, soak seeds in 122°F (50°C) water for 25 minutes prior to sowing.

SEED-STARTING SOIL TEMPERATURE: Optimal is 65–75°F (18–24°C) but seeds will germinate at 50°F (10°C).

SEED START TIMING: Start indoors 6–8 weeks before planting to allow seedlings time to harden off. Can plant in the garden a month prior to last frost date.

LIGHT REQUIREMENTS: As soon as seedlings emerge

TRANSPLANT: Plant one month prior to last frost.

DIRECT SOWING: Sow when soil temperatures reach 50°F (10°C).

GERMINATION: 7–15 days

DAYS TO MATURITY: Broccoli 55–98; brussels sprouts 92–120; cabbage 60–110; Chinese cabbage 45–70; cauliflower 50–85; collards 60–75; kale 30–65; kohlrabi 75–80; sprouting broccoli 80–130; rutabaga 80–90; Siberian kale 30–50; Swede 80; broccoli raab 50–60; turnip 30–60

POLLINATION: Insect

CROSS-POLLINATION: Can cross-pollinate with other varieties. Cage plants and introduce pollinators to prevent cross-pollination.

ISOLATION DISTANCE: 1 mile (1.6 km)

SEED MATURITY: Seeds mature the second year when siliques turn from green to brown. Dry on the plant.

SEED PROCESSING: Thresh

SEED VIABILITY: 5–7 years

Peppers
Capsicum spp.

Spicy or mild, lovely bells or scary ghosts, peppers belong in your garden. Not only are they delicious, they add a gorgeous pop of color to vegetable gardens. When starting pepper seeds, consider using a heat mat. Because peppers prefer warmth to germinate, start the seeds indoors about 8 weeks prior to last frost rather than direct sowing. Be patient. Peppers take their own sweet time before making an appearance. Transplant to a larger container when the first true leaves appear.

Peppers prefer rich, well-draining soil. Good calcium and phosphorus levels in the soil lead to higher yields. Although most peppers are self-fertile, wind or insects can cause cross-pollination. Bag or cage the plants to maintain pure seed. Also, stake pepper plants, as their heavy fruit can break a plant's fragile stem.

When saving seeds, the color of the pepper indicates maturity, as well as seed harvest time. Many peppers turn red when fully ripe, but different varieties achieve different coloration at maturity. While peppers generally may be harvested at any stage for culinary use, you need fully mature fruit for seed saving.

NOTE: Don't wait until the end of the season to save pepper seeds. When temperatures drop below 53°F (12°C), peppers will not set fruit. Additionally, evening temperatures between 55–60°F (13–16°C) lead to small fruits that don't contain viable seeds. Be certain to harvest mature peppers earlier in the season to save seeds.

Saving pepper seeds is simple: Slice open a fruit vertically and separate the seeds from the core. Spread the seeds on a paper plate and allow seeds to dry for two weeks. One important note when harvesting hot peppers: protect yourself! Wear gloves when processing and a mask if you're dehydrating peppers in the oven, as the fumes affect breathing. Do not touch your eyes when processing peppers!

↑ Sweet or spicy, peppers deserve a place in the garden.

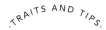

PEPPERS

COMMON NAME: Pepper

SCIENTIFIC NAME: *Capsicum* spp.

FAMILY: Solanaceae

LIFE CYCLE: Tender perennial treated as annual

FRUIT TYPE: Berry

SEED-STARTING DEPTH: ¼" (0.6 cm)

SPECIAL NEEDS: Use bottom heat.

SEED-STARTING SOIL TEMPERATURE: 70–85°F (21–29°C)

SEED START TIMING: 8 weeks prior to last frost

LIGHT REQUIREMENTS: As soon as seedlings emerge

TRANSPLANT: Plant after danger of frost. Space plants 18–24" (46–61 cm) apart and stake.

DIRECT SOWING: Not recommended

GERMINATION: 7–21 days

DAYS TO MATURITY: Sweet peppers 60–90; hot peppers up to 150.

POLLINATION: Self

CROSS-POLLINATION: Can cross-pollinate with other varieties. Cage plants or bag blossoms to prevent cross-pollination.

ISOLATION DISTANCE: 300–1,600' (91–488 m)

SEED MATURITY: Allow fruit to ripen fully to final color before harvesting seeds.

SEED PROCESSING: Remove from fruit and dry

SEED VIABILITY: 2–4 years

TOP 10 PEPPERS, SWEET AND HOT

I grow a lot of peppers, and although I'm a wimp with a pain tolerance of zero, I grow both sweet and hot peppers. Here are my favorites:

TOP 10 PRETTIEST, TASTIEST SWEET PEPPERS

'Purple Beauty'

'White Cloud'

'Violet Sparkle'

'Quadrato d'Asti Rosso'

'Tequila Sunrise'

'Orange Bell'

'Corno di Toro Giallo'

'Bullnose'

'Golden Marconi'

'Jimmy Nardello' Italian

TOP 10 MOST GORGEOUS, DEVILISHLY HOT PEPPERS

'Chinese 5-Color'

'Fish'

'Craig's Grande' Jalapeno

Thai Red Chili

Serrano Tampequino

'Trinidad Scorpion' (Yellow)

'Sante Fe Grande'

'Scotch Bonnet' (Yellow)

'Goat Horn'

'Carolina Reaper'

Endive, Escarole/Belgian Endive, Chicory, Italian Dandelion and Radicchio
Cichorium endivia, Cichorium intybus

It may seem tricky to navigate the world of *Cichorium endivia* versus *C. intybus*. However, these plants possess similar growing conditions. Both species prefer cool temperatures. Both require caging to avoid cross-pollination. Both may overwinter in gardens in mild climates, which will induce flowering and seed setting the second year. And both are much tastier and less expensive when grown at home than those found in a grocery store's produce section.

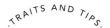

·TRAITS AND TIPS·

ENDIVE, ESCAROLE/BELGIAN ENDIVE, CHICORY, ITALIAN DANDELION, AND RADICCHIO

COMMON NAMES: Endive, escarole/Belgian endive, chicory, Italian dandelion, radicchio

SCIENTIFIC NAMES: *Cichorium endivia, Cichorium intybus*

FAMILY: Asteraceae

LIFE CYCLE: *C. endivia* annual; *C. intybus* biennial

FRUIT TYPE: Achene

SEED-STARTING DEPTH: ¼" (0.6 cm)

SPECIAL NEEDS: Belgian endive is unique. Grow it normally outdoors during its first season. Remove the outer leaves of the rosette and harvest the roots. Plant the roots in pots, placing in a dark location to grow inside. By not exposing the leaves to sunlight as the plant grows, the vegetable turns a creamy yellowish white, providing a mild, non-bitter flavor. The blanched leaves that form are what's harvested and eaten.

SEED-STARTING SOIL TEMPERATURE: 60–70°F (16–21°C)

SEED START TIMING: Direct sowing after frost is preferred. Can be started indoors 4–5 weeks before last frost.

LIGHT REQUIREMENTS: As soon as seedlings emerge

TRANSPLANT: Plants tolerate cool temperatures, dislike heat. In mild climates, plant in fall and overwinter in the garden for seed production its second season. Dig roots in cold climates, trim leaves to 2" (5 cm) above crown; overwinter in potting soil in 32–40°F (0–4°C).

DIRECT SOWING: Sow after danger of frost has passed and when temperatures reach 55°F (13°C).

GERMINATION: 5–7 days

DAYS TO MATURITY: 85–100

POLLINATION: Self (*Cichorium endivia*); insect (*Cichorium intybus*)

CROSS-POLLINATION: Can cross-pollinate with other varieties. Cage plants or bag blossoms to prevent cross-pollination. Introduce insects or hand-pollinate *Cichorium intybus*.

ISOLATION DISTANCE: 10–20' (3–6 m) *Cichorium endivia*; 800' (0.24 km) *Cichorium intybus*

SEED MATURITY: Seeds mature after market maturity, *Cichorium endivia*; second season after cold period, *Cichorium intybus*. Seeds are enclosed in dry flower bracts that may shatter.

SEED PROCESSING: Thresh

SEED VIABILITY: 6 years

Watermelon and Citron
Citrullus lanatus

Heirloom watermelons offer more options than the standard red flesh. White, yellow, orange, pink . . . so many options to grow in your garden! However, watermelon vines demand plenty of space. Also, for delicious, large melons, you need to cull the growing fruits so that only one or two remain on the vine. Citron melons look similar to watermelons, but the flesh is hard and the fruit is most often pickled.

To determine when to harvest the fruit, look at the color of the fruit's rind where it touches the ground. When it turns yellow, it's time to harvest. Also, another indicator is the tendril closest to the fruit. When it's dried and black, the fruit is ready to harvest.

WATERMELON AND CITRON

COMMON NAMES: Watermelon, citron

SCIENTIFIC NAME: *Citrullus lanatus*

FAMILY: Cucurbitaceae

LIFE CYCLE: Annual

FRUIT TYPE: Berry

SEED-STARTING DEPTH: 1" (3 cm)

SPECIAL NEEDS: Sow seeds in individual biodegradable pots when starting indoors. Avoid disturbing roots when planting in garden.

SEED-STARTING SOIL TEMPERATURE: 80–90°F (27–32°C)

SEED START TIMING: Start indoors 4 weeks prior to last frost. Bottom heat speeds germination.

LIGHT REQUIREMENTS: As soon as seedlings emerge

TRANSPLANT: Plant after danger of frost. Do not disturb roots. Plant in hills, one or two plants per hill, spaced 6–8' (2–2.5 m) apart.

DIRECT SOWING: Sow after danger of frost has passed and when temperatures reach 70–85°F (21–29°C).

GERMINATION: 3–10 days

DAYS TO MATURITY: 70–110 days from planting

POLLINATION: Insect

CROSS-POLLINATION: Can cross-pollinate with other varieties. Cage plants or bag blossoms to prevent cross-pollination. Hand-pollinate or introduce insects.

ISOLATION DISTANCE: 800'–½ mile (0.24–0.8 km)

SEED MATURITY: Same as fruit maturity. Save seeds from fruit with the best flavors, preferred shapes, and colors.

SEED PROCESSING: Rinse. Dry for 1 week.

SEED VIABILITY: 5 years

Cucumber and Melon
Cucumis sativus, Cucumis melo

Although heirloom cucumbers and melons take up a lot of garden real estate, they're worth the space investment. Unless you're growing a bush variety of cucumbers, grow up—create a trellis and train the vines around it. Even small melons grow well on a trellis as long as you support the heavy fruit with old nylons tied around them and secured to the trellis. Trellising not only saves space, it keeps the plants off the ground so you can more easily spot pests or diseases, and eases back pain when harvesting.

Both melons and cucumbers prefer warm temperatures, good air circulation, and consistent water. After all, these crops are 90 or 95 percent water, respectively. Don't skimp on the water. Feed cucumbers diluted fish emulsion each week. Melons prefer humus-rich soil.

The main difference in seed saving involves timing. Melon seeds reach maturity at the same time the fruit is ready to eat. Simply harvest the seeds before eating, separate from the pulp, rinse well, and dry. Cucumber seeds, though, require longer ripening time. Allow fruits to continue to ripen past their prime for at least 5 weeks, either on the vine or harvested and stored in a cool, dry place. Remove seeds from pulp, rinse well, and dry. Seeds can also be fermented.

↑ Growing heirlooms gives you the chance to try interesting varieties, like this Indian melon 'Kajari'.

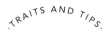

CUCUMBER AND MELON

COMMON NAMES: Cucumber, melon

SCIENTIFIC NAMES: *Cucumis sativus, Cucumis melo*

FAMILY: Cucurbitaceae

LIFE CYCLE: Annual

FRUIT TYPE: Fleshy

SEED-STARTING DEPTH: ½" (1.3 cm)

SPECIAL NEEDS: None

SEED-STARTING SOIL TEMPERATURE: 80–90°F (27–32°C)

SEED START TIMING: Start indoors using biodegradable containers 3–4 weeks before last frost. Bottom heat speeds germination.

LIGHT REQUIREMENTS: As soon as seedlings emerge

TRANSPLANT: Plant after danger of frost. Do not disturb roots. Prefers soils temperature 65–75°F (18–24°C). Space plants 8" (20 cm) apart if trellising, 4–5' (1–1.5 m) apart if letting plants sprawl.

DIRECT SOWING: Sow after danger of frost has passed and when temperatures reach 65°F (18°C).

GERMINATION: 3–10 days

DAYS TO MATURITY: 48–80 cucumbers; 70–100 melons

POLLINATION: Insect

CROSS-POLLINATION: Can cross-pollinate with other varieties but not between cucumbers and melons. Bag blossoms to prevent cross-pollination. Hand-pollinate. (First flowers are most commonly male; wait until female flowers appear.)

ISOLATION DISTANCE: 800'–½ mile (0.24–0.8 km)

SEED MATURITY: Harvest cucumber seed 5 weeks after fruit's edible maturity, when it changes color to yellow, white, orange, or brown. Harvest melon seed when fruit is ripe for eating.

SEED PROCESSING: Rinse or ferment (cucumber); rinse (melon)

SEED VIABILITY: 5 years

Pumpkin, Winter and Summer Squash, and Gourd
Cucurbita spp.

Ah, pumpkins and squashes, the bullies of the garden. They're terrible space hogs and will run over any pretty companion plants you add to their beds. But no matter what their bullying habits are, I always invite them to the garden party because they're pretty and delicious. They can also be prima donnas, demanding constant attention to prevent damage by pests and disease. Why do we persist? Because there's nothing more fun than growing your own jack o'lanterns, that's why! When your autumn decorations include a tableful of gourds and miniature pumpkins, and you've carved silly faces into those large, orange fruit, all the *Cucurbita* angst is forgotten.

HOW TO CONTROL SQUASH VINE BORERS

Squash vine borers are my nemesis. The larvae from the orange-and-black sesiid moth *Melittia satyriniformis* burrow into the stem of a squash plant, eating it from the inside. You'll know you have squash vine borers if you find your plants suffering a sudden collapse; the plant looks wilted, but the soil is still moist. It's so frustrating!

However, a few years ago, I read about a companion planting technique that involves icicle radishes. Plant three to five icicle radishes in close proximity to each squash plant. Don't harvest the radish. Instead, allow it to mature and flower. The radish blooms repel the moths, encouraging them to lay eggs elsewhere. As an organic gardener, I like to try every alternative before using chemicals of any kind. Diatomaceous earth is also safe to use to prevent squash vine borers. Most important, check the plants daily for eggs on the leaves (check undersides as well). Removal of eggs is crucial to preventing plant death by squash vine borer.

Summer squash tastes best when it's harvested young and tender. Baseball bat-sized zucchini found late in the season, hidden under foliage, are not delicious. However, they may be good for seed saving, as squash needs to be past its preferred harvest time for seed maturity. (When the rind is hard to pierce with a fingernail, the seeds should be mature.)

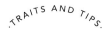

PUMPKIN, WINTER AND SUMMER SQUASH, AND GOURD

COMMON NAMES: Pumpkin, winter squash, summer squash, gourd

SCIENTIFIC NAMES: *Cucurbita pepo, Cucurbita moschata, Cucurbita maxima,* and *Cucurbita mixta*

FAMILY: Cucurbitaceae

LIFE CYCLE: Annual

FRUIT TYPE: Fleshy (pepo)

SEED-STARTING DEPTH: 1" (3 cm)

SPECIAL NEEDS: Beware squash vine borer. Companion plant icicle radishes among squash vines to deter this pest.

SEED-STARTING SOIL TEMPERATURE: 70–95°F (21–35°C)

SEED START TIMING: Start indoors using biodegradable containers 4–5 weeks before last frost.

LIGHT REQUIREMENTS: As soon as seedlings emerge

TRANSPLANT: Plant after danger of frost. Do not disturb roots. Plant 8" (20 cm) apart if trellising, 4' (1.2 m) apart if sprawling.

DIRECT SOWING: Sow after danger of frost has passed and when soil temperature reaches 60°F (16°C).

GERMINATION: 5–10 days

DAYS TO MATURITY: 43–75 summer squash; 85–110 winter squash; 100–115 pumpkin; 95–125 gourd

POLLINATION: Insect

CROSS-POLLINATION: Can cross-pollinate with other varieties. Bag blossoms to prevent cross-pollination. Hand-pollinate.

ISOLATION DISTANCE: 800'–½ mile (0.24–0.8 km)

SEED MATURITY: Harvest seeds approximately 4 weeks after fruit maturity.

SEED PROCESSING: Rinse

SEED VIABILITY: 4 years

Artichoke and Cardoon
Cynara cardunculus

While artichokes are grown for their edible immature inflorescences and bracts, cardoons' edible portion is the leaf petiole or stalk, which is peeled and blanched before eating. Both plants produce stunning flowers but require vernalization for blooms and seed setting. They will cross-pollinate with each other, so bag blooms and hand-pollinate using a brush. (Gather pollen from the base of the flower on the brush, transfer to the stigmas, and replace the bag. Repeat over the next several days to ensure pollination. Keep the bag in place until flowering is finished.)

Cardoons are grown as an annual for culinary use, but to save seeds, it must be grown as a perennial or, at least, a biennial. Sacrifice a few plants for seed production rather than culinary use. Artichokes continue to produce flowers and seeds for 3 to 6 years, depending on the variety. Both plants are large—give them adequate space in the garden, at least 3' (91 cm).

ARTICHOKE AND CARDOON

COMMON NAMES: Artichoke, cardoon

SCIENTIFIC NAME: *Cynara cardunculus* var. *scolymus*; *Cynara cardunculus* var. *altilis*

FAMILY: Asteraceae

LIFE CYCLE: Perennial in mild climates; annual in cold climates

FRUIT TYPE: Dry, indehiscent, single-seeded

SEED-STARTING DEPTH: ½" (1.3 cm)

SPECIAL NEEDS: Soak seeds overnight to boost germination.

SEED-STARTING SOIL TEMPERATURE: 70–75°F (21–24°C)

SEED START TIMING: Start indoors using biodegradable containers 8–10 weeks before last frost.

LIGHT REQUIREMENTS: As soon as seedlings emerge

TRANSPLANT: Plant after danger of frost when air temperatures reach at least 60°F (16°C). Space 4' (1.2 m) apart.

DIRECT SOWING: Not recommended

GERMINATION: 10–21 days

DAYS TO MATURITY: 110–150

POLLINATION: Insect

CROSS-POLLINATION: Can cross-pollinate with other varieties. Cage plants or bag blossoms to prevent cross-pollination. Hand-pollinate.

ISOLATION DISTANCE: 800'–½ mile (0.24–0.8 km)

SEED MATURITY: Seeds mature 60 days after fertilization. Seeds mature when bracts turn from green to brown and light gray pappuses emerge from seedheads.

SEED PROCESSING: Thresh; winnow to remove seeds from chaff.

SEED VIABILITY: 6 years

Carrot
Daucus carota

Carrots seem like they should be an easy garden crop, don't they? Unfortunately, they're finicky about their soil and placement. Carrots require vernalization to flower and produce seeds. In warm climates, overwinter the crop in the garden, mulching well. In cold areas, dig the roots in autumn before the ground freezes and store in cool, humid location at 35°F (2°C). Place roots in damp sand. Replant in spring 6–18" (15–46 cm) apart for seed production. (For food production, carrots can grow with 1–2" (3–5 cm) spacing between them.)

CARROT

COMMON NAME: Carrot

SCIENTIFIC NAME: *Daucus carota*

FAMILY: Apiaceae

LIFE CYCLE: Biennial

FRUIT TYPE: Schizocarps split at maturity into two single-seeded, indehiscent mericaps.

SEED-STARTING DEPTH: ¼–½" (0.6–1.3 cm)

SPECIAL NEEDS: Seeds are slow to germinate.

SEED-STARTING SOIL TEMPERATURE: 50–85°F (10–29°C)

SEED START TIMING: Direct sowing after frost is preferred.

LIGHT REQUIREMENTS: As soon as seedlings emerge

TRANSPLANT: Sow seeds after danger of frost in shallow rows. Replant vernalized roots in spring, 6–18" (15–46 cm) apart.

DIRECT SOWING: Sow after danger of frost has passed and when temperatures reach 55°F (13°C).

GERMINATION: 7–21 days

DAYS TO MATURITY: 70–80

POLLINATION: Insect

CROSS-POLLINATION: Can cross-pollinate with other varieties, as well as Queen Anne's Lace, which is considered a wild carrot. Cage plants or bag blossoms to prevent cross-pollination. Introduce pollinators or hand-pollinate.

ISOLATION DISTANCE: 800'–½ mile (0.24–0.8 km)

SEED MATURITY: 4–6 weeks post pollination. Umbellets turn brown, indicating mature seeds. Primary umbellets mature first, then secondary. (Typically, primary umbellets contain the best seeds.) Harvest a whole umbel and hang it upside down to dry or bag an umbel on plants in the garden to avoid seed loss due to shattering. Continue drying 1–3 weeks. Cure seeds 4–5 days in hot, dry conditions or 2 weeks in humid areas.

SEED PROCESSING: Hang or place in a bag and flail. Winnow to remove debris.

SEED VIABILITY: 6 years

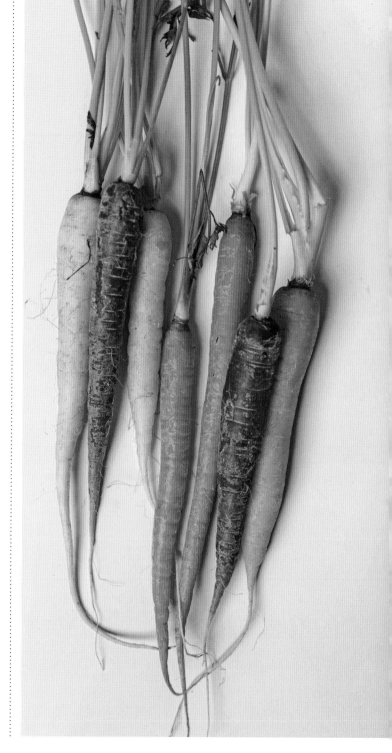

→ A rainbow of carrots

Arugula (Rocket, Roquette)
Eruca sativa

Arugula is an easy crop to grow, although it does get quite spicy if exposed to high temperatures. To save arugula seeds, allow the plant to bolt in the heat of summer. You can also harvest a few edible flowers to enhance your fancy culinary game but allow the rest of the blooms to set seed.

·TRAITS AND TIPS·

ARUGULA

COMMON NAMES: Arugula, rocket, roquette

SCIENTIFIC NAME: *Eruca sativa*

FAMILY: Brassicaceae

LIFE CYCLE: Annual

FRUIT TYPE: Silique

SEED-STARTING DEPTH: ¼" (0.6 cm)

SPECIAL NEEDS: It doesn't transplant well. If started indoors, use biodegradable pots.

SEED-STARTING SOIL TEMPERATURE: 60–77°F (16–25°C)

SEED START TIMING: Direct sowing after frost is preferred. Can be started indoors using biodegradable containers 4 weeks before last frost.

LIGHT REQUIREMENTS: As soon as seedlings emerge

TRANSPLANT: Plant after danger of frost. Do not disturb roots. If growing for seed, increase spacing to 6" (15 cm) between plants.

DIRECT SOWING: Sow after danger of frost has passed and when temperatures reach 60°F (16°C).

GERMINATION: 5–7 days

DAYS TO MATURITY: 45–60

POLLINATION: Insect

CROSS-POLLINATION: Can cross-pollinate with other varieties. Cage plants or bag blossoms to prevent cross-pollination. Introduce pollinators into cages or hand-pollinate.

ISOLATION DISTANCE: 800'–½ mile (0.24–0.8 km)

SEED MATURITY: Dry silique on the plant or harvest entire plants and hang them upside down to dry.

SEED PROCESSING: Thresh. Do not damage seed coat.

SEED VIABILITY: 6 years

Edamame and Soybean
Glycine max

Popular for its snack appeal, edamame is also an easy crop to grow for new seed savers. Edamame is self-pollinating, the seeds are large and easy to clean, and flowers are typically pollinated before they open, reducing the risk of cross-pollination. Edamame tolerates light frost. Allow pods to dry on the plant for seed harvest. Wear gloves when harvesting, as pods are sharp.

EDAMAME AND SOYBEAN

COMMON NAMES: Edamame, soybean

SCIENTIFIC NAME: *Glycine max*

FAMILY: Fabaceae

LIFE CYCLE: Annual

FRUIT TYPE: Dry, dehiscent (legume)

SEED-STARTING DEPTH: 1" (3 cm)

SPECIAL NEEDS: It prefers compost-rich soil.

SEED-STARTING SOIL TEMPERATURE: 60–75°F (16–24°C)

SEED START TIMING: Direct sowing after frost is preferred.

LIGHT REQUIREMENTS: As soon as seedlings emerge

TRANSPLANT: Not recommended

DIRECT SOWING: Sow after danger of frost has passed and when temperatures reach 60°F (16°C).

GERMINATION: 5–7 days

DAYS TO MATURITY: 75–110. Harvest immature plants for eating.

POLLINATION: Self

CROSS-POLLINATION: None

ISOLATION DISTANCE: 10–20' (3–6 m)

SEED MATURITY: Dry pods on plants. Harvest when a pod turns from green to tan.

SEED PROCESSING: Thresh gently to avoid damaging seeds. Winnow to remove chaff.

SEED VIABILITY: 3–4 years

Lettuce
Lactuca sativa

Speckled, freckled, ruffled, red, green with red edging . . . heirloom lettuces look different than the round, pale, crunchy iceberg lettuce I grew up eating. Lettuce prefers cool temperatures, otherwise it will bolt and become bitter. Be careful when harvesting seed from early flowers, as you're inadvertently selecting seeds from a parent plant with the tendency to bolt early, which is not ideal.

Newly harvested seeds undergo a period of dormancy. Wait at least two months prior to planting for germination success. Additionally, if seeds are exposed to temperatures greater than 77°F (25°C), seeds become dormant and require a cold treatment period before germinating. Hold the seeds in a cool basement or cellar with temperatures ranging from 50 to 59°F (10 to 15°C). As if those issues aren't enough to challenge a gardener, some lettuce varieties need exposure to light to germinate. Still, while there are a few challenges to consider when growing lettuce, homegrown heirloom lettuce is worth the extra effort. (Keep plants well watered and plant early to avoid heat. For leaf lettuce, you can harvest outer leaves while allowing the plant to continue to grow, extending your harvest time.)

TOP 10 PRETTIEST, TASTIEST LETTUCES

- 'Forellenschluss'
- 'Devil's Ear'
- 'Flash Butter Oak'
- 'Flame'
- 'Lollo Rossa'
- 'Rouge d'Hiver'
- 'Merveille des Quartre Saisons'
- 'Pablo'
- 'Garnet Rose'
- 'Bronze Beauty'

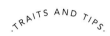

TRAITS AND TIPS

LETTUCE

COMMON NAME: Lettuce

SCIENTIFIC NAME: *Lactuca sativa*

FAMILY: Asteraceae

LIFE CYCLE: Annual

FRUIT TYPE: Achene

SEED-STARTING DEPTH: ¼" (0.6 cm)

SPECIAL NEEDS: Requires light for germination. Do not plant freshly harvested seeds as they will not germinate; hold for 2-plus months.

SEED-STARTING SOIL TEMPERATURE: 70–75°F (21–24°C)

SEED START TIMING: Direct sowing after frost is preferred. Can be started indoors using biodegradable containers 4–5 weeks before last frost. Can succession plant by sowing seeds indoors every few weeks to replace harvested lettuce.

LIGHT REQUIREMENTS: It needs light to germinate. As seedlings emerge, continue 12–16 hours of light per day.

TRANSPLANT: Plant after danger of frost. Space 12" (30 cm) apart for larger heading varieties, 6" (15 cm) apart for smaller leaf lettuces. Increase spacing to 15" (38 cm) for seed saving as plants will grow large.

DIRECT SOWING: Sow after danger of frost has passed and when temperatures reach 55°F (13°C).

GERMINATION: 2–12 days

DAYS TO MATURITY: Depends on variety: 45–55 for looseleaf; 75–100 for heading lettuce

POLLINATION: Self

CROSS-POLLINATION: Can cross-pollinate with wild varieties but not a big concern as it self-pollinates.

ISOLATION DISTANCE: 10–20' (3–6 m)

SEED MATURITY: After edible harvest maturity. Allow plants to bolt. Seeds are mature when the pappuses appear. Collect seeds before they're dispersed by wind by handpicking or bagging plants and shaking seeds into a bag.

SEED PROCESSING: Screen to remove chaff

SEED VIABILITY: 6 years

Parsnip
Pastinaca sativa

Parsnips provide a great benefit: They can withstand cold temperatures better than almost every vegetable in the garden. However, they also cause a bit of pain, as the leaves and stems produce a sap that can cause a nasty rash. So, handle parsnips with care; wear gloves to avoid the sap.

Grown much like carrots but with a longer tolerance for cold, parsnips produce sweeter flavors when they're kissed by cold weather. In fact, you can leave the roots in the ground all winter without damage. (Harvesting parsnips as needed in the winter can be challenging, though, chiseling through frozen soil.) The ability to withstand the cold benefits seed savers, as there's no need to dig the roots to induce vernalization. Add a layer of mulch to the crop and leave it in the garden to overwinter. After its exposure to cold, the plants will be ready to flower and produce seeds in the spring. Bag the blossoms, as parsnips cross-pollinate. Parsnip seeds don't last. Use fresh seed each season.

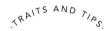

TRAITS AND TIPS.

PARSNIP

COMMON NAME: Parsnip

SCIENTIFIC NAME: *Pastinaca sativa*

FAMILY: Apiaceae

LIFE CYCLE: Biennial

FRUIT TYPE: Schizocarps split at maturity into two indehiscent mericarps.

SEED-STARTING DEPTH: ½" (1.3 cm)

SPECIAL NEEDS: Plants require vernalization of 10 weeks below 50°F (10 C) to produce seeds. Use only fresh seeds each season.

SEED-STARTING SOIL TEMPERATURE: 50–54°F (10–12°C)

SEED START TIMING: Direct sowing after frost is preferred.

LIGHT REQUIREMENTS: As soon as seedlings emerge

TRANSPLANT: Not recommended; direct sow in the garden.

DIRECT SOWING: Sow after danger of frost has passed and temperatures reach 55°F (13°C).

GERMINATION: 14–21 days

DAYS TO MATURITY: 120

POLLINATION: Insect

CROSS-POLLINATION: Can cross-pollinate with wild parsnip. Cage plants or bag blossoms to prevent cross-pollination.

ISOLATION DISTANCE: 800'–½ mile (0.24–0.8 km)

SEED MATURITY: Seeds change from green to tan as they mature. Gather seedheads when approximately two-thirds of an umbel has turned brown, and continue to dry.

SEED PROCESSING: Thresh

SEED VIABILITY: 1 year

Bean
Phaseolus vulgaris (common), *Phaseolus coccineus* (runner), *Vicia faba* (fava), *Phaseolus lunatus* (lima), *Cicer arietinum* (chickpea), *Vigna unguiculata* (cowpea)

Purple, yellow, speckled, foot-long, bush, green, pole . . . the varieties seem endless. And whether you prefer beans fresh in the pod or dried, you've never met a more versatile vegetable. Now, here's the thing: there are many bean varieties and classifications. However, they grow from seed similarly, and seed harvesting is similar as well, which is why I've grouped all the beans into one section.

Like tomatoes, bean varieties range from determinate (bush), indeterminate (pole or runner), and semi-determinate (half-runner). Your garden space might dictate the type you grow. I love runner beans because I trellis the vines in the garden, which saves space—and my back when harvesting. However, if your space is limited or you prefer container gardening, bush beans may be a better option. Determinate beans flower, produce fruit, and reach maturity in a short amount of time, while indeterminate beans flower and continue to produce fruit throughout the life of the plant. If you plan to process beans for canning or freezing, bush varieties are a good choice for efficiency.

Grow beans in a sunny location in well-drained soil that's rich in organic matter. Bean plants add nitrogen to the soil, which is beneficial to crops that require nitrogen to produce well, like corn. Consider companion planting with crops that can benefit from a nitrogen boost. As beans grow throughout the season, add compost as a sidedressing or fertilize with kelp to keep the plants well fed. Water well, particularly as plants become established and blooms begin to appear.

Pest alert: Beans attract all kinds of undesirables, like Japanese beetles, aphids, striped cucumber beetles, and Mexican bean beetles. Row covers help prevent infestations, but vigilant handpicking and squishing is always a good remedy. Check your plants often before a pest population gets out of control.

Continuous harvest of indeterminate beans for fresh eating helps the plant to produce well all season. Harvest beans for fresh eating when they are young and tender. To save seeds or to harvest dry beans, however, allow the pods to dry on the vine until they turn yellowish tan, approximately 6 weeks after the beans are ready for fresh eating.

TOP 10
DELICIOUS AND GORGEOUS
BEAN VARIETIES

- 'Purple Podded' (Pole)
- 'Dragon Tongue' (Bush)
- 'Cherokee Trail of Tears' (Pole)
- 'Calima' (Bush)
- 'Painted Lady' (Runner)
- 'Thai Purple Podded' Yard-Long Beans
- 'Old Homestead' (Also known as 'Kentucky Wonder' Pole. In fact, there are nine common names associated with this old heirloom bean.)
- 'Meraviglia di Venezia' (Bush)
- 'Rattlesnake' (Pole)
- 'Christmas Lima' (Pole)

TRAITS AND TIPS

BEAN

COMMON NAMES: Common bean, French bean, green bean, haricot, snap bean, string bean

SCIENTIFIC NAME: *Phaseolus vulgaris*

FAMILY: Fabaceae

LIFE CYCLE: Annual

DAYS TO MATURITY: 70–80 pole; 65–75 bush

COMMON NAME: Runner bean

SCIENTIFIC NAME: *Phaseolus coccineus*

FAMILY: Fabaceae

LIFE CYCLE: Perennial grown as an annual

DAYS TO MATURITY: 45–55

COMMON NAMES: Fava bean, broad bean, English bean, European bean, field bean

SCIENTIFIC NAME: *Vicia faba*

FAMILY: Fabaceae

LIFE CYCLE: Annual

DAYS TO MATURITY: 80–100

COMMON NAMES: Lima bean, butter bean, civet, Carolina, sewee

SCIENTIFIC NAME: *Phaseolus lunatus*

FAMILY: Fabaceae

LIFE CYCLE: Annual

DAYS TO MATURITY: 60–80 bush; 85–90 pole

COMMON NAMES: Chickpea, garbanzo, Egyptian pea

SCIENTIFIC NAME: *Cicer arietinum*

FAMILY: Fabaceae

LIFE CYCLE: Annual

DAYS TO MATURITY: 100

COMMON NAME: Tepary bean

SCIENTIFIC NAME: *Phaseolus acutifolius*

FAMILY: Fabaceae

LIFE CYCLE: Annual

DAYS TO MATURITY: 75–85

ALL

FRUIT TYPE: Dehiscent legume or pod

SEED-STARTING DEPTH: 1" (3 cm)

SPECIAL NEEDS: None

SEED-STARTING SOIL TEMPERATURE: 60–85°F (16–29°C)

SEED START TIMING: Direct sowing 1–2 weeks after frost is preferred. Can be started indoors using biodegradable containers 4 weeks before last frost.

LIGHT REQUIREMENTS: As soon as seedlings emerge

TRANSPLANT: Plant after danger of frost. Space bush varieties 24" (61 cm) apart, runner/pole varieties 10" (25 cm) apart, and trellis.

DIRECT SOWING: Sow after danger of frost has passed and when soil temperatures reach 60°F (16°C).

GERMINATION: 8–10 days

POLLINATION: Self except for runner beans, which are insect-pollinated. There's small chance of cross-pollination among other beans.

CROSS-POLLINATION: Small chance of cross-pollinating with other varieties. Cage plants or bag blossoms to prevent cross-pollination.

ISOLATION DISTANCE: 10–20' (3–6 m) common, tepary; 160–500' (49–152 m) lima, runner

SEED MATURITY: Dry pods on plants or harvest prior to frost and allow pods to continue to dry fully.

SEED PROCESSING: Hand process or flail gently.

SEED VIABILITY: 3–4 years

Tomatillo and Ground Cherry
Physalis philadelphica, Physalis grisea

Tomatillos and ground cherries are the perfect little garden presents. Wrapped neatly in their husks, growing prettily until ripe, when the wrapping bursts open and provides us with a tasty gift. Like tomatoes, the seeds of both tomatillos and ground cherries ripen at the same time as the fruit, which makes harvesting easy. When the husk splits is the perfect time to harvest tomatillos. Ground cherries live up to their name—they literally drop to the ground when they're ripe.

TOMATILLO AND GROUND CHERRY

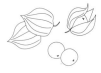

COMMON NAMES: Tomatillo, ground cherry

SCIENTIFIC NAMES: *Physalis philadelphica, Physalis grisea*

FAMILY: Solanaceae

LIFE CYCLE: Annual

FRUIT TYPE: Berry

SEED-STARTING DEPTH: ¼" (0.6 cm)

SPECIAL NEEDS: They prefer bottom heat for germination.

SEED-STARTING SOIL TEMPERATURE: 75–90°F (24–32°C)

SEED START TIMING: Start indoors 4–6 weeks before last frost. Bottom heat speeds germination.

LIGHT REQUIREMENTS: As soon as seedlings emerge

TRANSPLANT: Plant after danger of frost. Space 36" (91 cm) apart and support with stakes or cages.

DIRECT SOWING: In long, warm-season climates, sow after danger of frost has passed and when temperatures reach 60°F (16°C).

GERMINATION: 7–14 days

DAYS TO MATURITY: 65–80

POLLINATION: Self

CROSS-POLLINATION: Can cross-pollinate with other varieties. Cage plants or bag blossoms to prevent cross-pollination.

ISOLATION DISTANCE: 800'–½ mile (0.24–0.8 km) tomatillo; 300–1,600' (91–488 m) ground cherry

SEED MATURITY: Mature at edible stage when husks split.

SEED PROCESSING: Wet process; blend or mash and wash.

SEED VIABILITY: 4–6 years

Pea
Pisum sativum

Not only are peas delicious when eaten fresh, but pea blooms add a beautiful burst of delicate color to the garden. Peas are divided into two categories: garden and field. Garden peas are eaten fresh and include snap and snow peas, which have an edible, low-fiber pod, as well as shelling peas, which have a high-fiber pod that's traditionally not eaten. Saving seeds from garden peas requires the fruit continues to ripen past the edible green stage, allowing the pods to dry on the plant. Field peas, however, reach full maturity before they're harvested, with its peas typically used in soups. Field peas saved for seeds are harvested at the same time as for food.

Peas provide a perfect introduction for beginning seed starters and savers, as they're simple to grow, self-pollinate, and harvest and clean easily. The biggest trick with peas is to start them early, before summer's heat shuts down production. While direct sowing is optimal, I also start peas in biodegradable pots. Peas don't like their roots disturbed, so plant the entire pot in the garden. Most peas require trellising.

↑ With edible pods, tendrils, and flowers, there's much to love about peas.

PEA

COMMON NAMES: Pea, garden pea, snap pea, snow pea, shelling pea, field pea

SCIENTIFIC NAME: *Pisum sativum*

FAMILY: Fabaceae

LIFE CYCLE: Annual

FRUIT TYPE: Dry, dehiscent legume

SEED-STARTING DEPTH: 1" (3 cm)

SPECIAL NEEDS: Soak seeds overnight prior to planting.

SEED-STARTING SOIL TEMPERATURE: 40–75°F (4–24°C)

SEED START TIMING: Direct sow 2–3 weeks before last frost or when the soil is workable. Can be started indoors using biodegradable containers 4–5 weeks before last frost.

LIGHT REQUIREMENTS: As soon as seedlings emerge

TRANSPLANT: Plant two weeks prior to last frost. Do not disturb roots. Plant biodegradable containers in the garden. Space 4" (10 cm) apart, and trellis plants.

DIRECT SOWING: Sow 2–3 weeks prior to last frost and when soil temperatures reach 40°F (4°C).

GERMINATION: 7–14 days

DAYS TO MATURITY: 60–70 garden; 90–100 field

POLLINATION: Self

CROSS-POLLINATION: Self-pollinated. May rarely cross through insect pollination. Cage plants or bag blossoms to prevent cross-pollination.

ISOLATION DISTANCE: 10–20' (3–6 m)

SEED MATURITY: Dry pods on the plants.

SEED PROCESSING: Hand-shell or thresh

SEED VIABILITY: 3–4 years

Radish
Raphanus sativus

Growing radishes is easy—they prefer cool weather and need little space, about 4–6" (10–15 cm) between plants. However, growing radishes for seed is a bit trickier, as they do love to cross-pollinate, and they require a larger space to mature as the flower stalks can reach 4' (1 m) high. Additionally, biennial winter radishes, like daikon varieties, require vernalization before flowering and setting seed. However, most daikon radishes tolerate temperatures down to 25°F (-4°C) and can overwinter in the garden if mulched well. In colder climates, dig the roots and store in a cool root cellar, basement, or refrigerator. Replant the roots in the spring, spaced 12–18" (30–46 cm) apart.

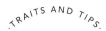

RADISH

COMMON NAMES: Radish, daikon, winter radish

SCIENTIFIC NAME: *Raphanus sativus*

FAMILY: Brassicaceae

LIFE CYCLE: Annual or biennial

FRUIT TYPE: Dry, dehiscent (silique)

SEED-STARTING DEPTH: ¼" (0.6 cm)

SPECIAL NEEDS: None

SEED-STARTING SOIL TEMPERATURE: 50–65°F (10–18°C)

SEED START TIMING: Direct sow 2–3 weeks prior to last frost.

LIGHT REQUIREMENTS: As soon as seedlings emerge

TRANSPLANT: Not recommended

DIRECT SOWING: Sow 2–3 weeks before last frost and when temperatures reach 50°F (10°C).

GERMINATION: 4–12 days

DAYS TO MATURITY: 22–70, depending on variety

POLLINATION: Insect

CROSS-POLLINATION: Can cross-pollinate with other varieties. Cage plants or bag blossoms to prevent cross-pollination. Introduce pollinators into cages.

ISOLATION DISTANCE: 800'–½ mile (0.24–0.8 km)

SEED MATURITY: After edible maturity. Dry pods on plants or harvest prior to frost and allow pods to continue to dry fully.

SEED PROCESSING: Thresh

SEED VIABILITY: 6 years

← A rainbow of options are available for tomatoes—no need to settle for simple red varieties.

Tomato
Solanum lycopersicum

Red, pink, orange, purple, striped, ribbed, miniscule, mammoth . . . tomatoes provide an abundance of color and texture on a dinner plate and add beauty to the garden. Many a gardener has been born thanks to the tomato: It starts with the craving for a taste of just-picked, sun-warmed tomato, and the next thing you know, you've got a garden full of them! For most gardeners, tomatoes are also the gateway to the seed-starting and -saving club. Saving the seeds of just one tomato can provide you with plants for many years to come.

Before You Begin

Start by evaluating your garden space. Each tomato plant needs approximately a 24-inch (61cm) circumference if you plan to stake/support the vine, which I highly recommend. Staking prevents diseases and saves your back when harvesting. If you plan to use containers for your tomatoes, you'll need space for 5-gallon (19 L) pots. However, you can also find several heirloom dwarf varieties that produce well in smaller spaces. Before you buy seeds, assess your garden and determine your available space.

Also note the amount of sun in various areas of your garden. Most large, beefsteak-type tomatoes need 6 to 8 hours of sunlight to produce healthy fruit. However, if your garden doesn't bask in full sun, don't worry—some smaller, cherry-type tomatoes will produce with less sun, particularly the yellow and white varieties.

Next, consider how you want to use your tomatoes. Do you desire a summer-long daily serving of bruschetta, or do you plan to preserve jars of sauce for winter? For a long season of tomato treats, *indeterminate* tomato plants provide continuous fruit throughout the growing season until frost or disease kills the vines. Indeterminate tomato plants need space and support, as the vines can grow as tall as 10 feet (3 m). For a crop that produces all at once in a big flush of fruit, *determinate* tomatoes provide a nice crop for canning and preserving. Plus, the vine is more manageable in containers, with the plant growing approximately 3 feet (1 m). For smaller spaces, dwarf tomato varieties offer short vines with decent production, perfect for containers on patios or balcony gardens.

Starting Tomato Seeds

Once you've assessed your garden, it's time for the fun to begin: selecting your seeds. With so many options, it's challenging to choose. Try chatting with tomato growers at a farmers' market to learn what varieties grow well in your area. The market is also a good resource to taste-test varieties. Not only can you buy a few heirloom tomatoes from your local farmer to taste and determine your preferences, you can save seeds from these heirloom tomatoes for next season's garden. (Be certain to ask the variety names so that you can properly label the seeds.)

↑ Share a few homegrown beauties, and soon neighbors will think you're a master gardener.

I grow a lot of tomatoes, so I use a 128-cell seed-starting flat filled with moistened soilless seed-starting mix. Some growers crowd dozens of seeds per cell, but I find it weakens the seedlings and makes transplanting difficult. Instead, place two or three tomato seeds per cell on top of the mix, then cover lightly with more mix—about ¼ inch (0.6 cm). Using a spray bottle, water the flat carefully to settle the seeds. Cover with a plastic dome.

To heat or not to heat: Tomato seeds germinate more quickly with the addition of bottom heat. A heat mat intended for seed starting provides a perfect addition to your gardening toolkit, as it offers consistent bottom heat to maintain an 80°F (27°C) soil temperature beneficial to tomato seed germination.

Light is right: While light isn't necessary to spur germination of tomato seeds, it is important once the cotyledon appear. Place the tray under a direct light source. (See page 28 for instructions on how to build an inexpensive seed-starting station.) Raise the lights as the plants grow.

Ideally, the lights should remain just an inch or two above the seedlings to avoid the plants becoming leggy—where a seedling stretches toward a light source, weakening its stem. Placing direct light immediately above the seedlings keep the plants compact and sturdy.

Offer a drink, but don't drown: Ensure the soilless mix stays moist but not soggy. I add a bit of water to the bottom tray, allowing the plants to absorb water from below as needed. I also spritz the flat using a spray bottle. Be certain the flats don't dry out, because you can lose your seedlings. Set a daily reminder on your phone if you're afraid you'll forget to water.

Bully the babies: To create vigorous tomato seedlings, give them a shake. It seems counterintuitive to mistreat your sweet little seedlings, but a twice-daily brushing or agitation of the plants with your hand helps strengthen seedlings' stems. (If you've handled any diseased plants, don't touch your seedlings until your hands are clean!)

↑ Biodegradable pots can be planted directly in the garden.

↑ Be gentle but don't worry; tomato seedlings are tougher than they look.

Move up: Once the tomato seedlings' true leaves appear, it's time for the babies to move into a new home. Any clean, sterilized, repurposed container will do but select one that gives the seedling room to stretch its roots. The biodegradable pots I use are 3 inches (8 cm) in diameter, don't require sterilizing, and can be planted directly into the garden without disturbing the plant's roots.

After the seedlings are out of their seed-starting cell, it's easy to gently tease the roots apart with your fingers, separating the plants. Prefill containers with a good organic potting mix, adding it to each container until it's about three-fourths full. Using your index finger, create a hole in the soil in the center of the container. It speeds the process to prefill several flats of containers so that the seedlings can be quickly transplanted without drying out. Insert a tomato seedling's roots into the hole and bury a portion of the stem. Add more potting soil until the soil line is about

an inch under a plant's first set of leaves. Firm the soil in the container, and water well to settle the plant. Place the plants back under the grow lights.

.NOTE.

The best tool I've found to transplant seedlings is an old kitchen fork. It fits perfectly into the individual cell, allowing the seedlings to be lifted without disturbing the roots.

Feed them right: Now's the time to give your tomato seedlings a bit of nutrition, particularly if yellow leaves appear or the stems look unnaturally purple, which can indicate a phosphorous deficiency. I water with a manure compost tea once a week until it's time to plant the tomatoes in the garden. Composted manure tea is gentle, adds nutrients to the soil, and doesn't damage young plants. Too much fertilizer can cause quick, lanky growth or even damage leaves due to the uptake of excessive nitrogen salts, causing more harm than good for the plant. If you choose to use biodegradable pots, you'll eventually see the tomato's roots growing through the pot. The pots will decompose naturally in the soil.

Hardening off: As your tomatoes grow and the danger of frost passes, it's time to prepare the plants for their permanent home. (See page 44 for details about hardening off seedlings.)

By the end of the 2-week hardening off period, the plants should be exposed to the same conditions as they will experience in the garden—full sun for 6–8 hours or more per day. By gradually introducing tomato plants to direct sunlight, you'll avoid sunscald (burning the plants' leaves). Young plants are similar to people in a way: after we've lounged around inside all winter, we need to protect our skin before heading to the beach.

Growing Conditions

Tomatoes require 6–8 hours of full sun for the best production. Good soil drainage is essential, as is a nearby water source. Avoid planting tomatoes near walnut trees, as tomatoes are sensitive to the juglone toxin exuded by the tree's roots.

Space plants 24 inches (61 cm) apart. Plant your tomatoes deep. Dig a hole and bury most of the stem, leaving about an inch of stem exposed between the soil line and the first set of leaves. If a plant became leggy while awaiting the last frost date, dig a trench and plant the tomato horizontally, laying the stem in the trench and gently guiding the leafy portion of the stem to curve upwards. Roots will grow along the buried stem, stabilizing the plant, while the leafy

portion will begin growing vertically toward the light. Add a layer of mulch to preserve soil moisture and prevent soil from splashing on plants when watering. When the plant reaches 18 inches (46 cm), begin staking. Continue tying up the plant as it grows.

Tomatoes are heavy feeders. Avoid adding too much nitrogen in the soil, as it will promote foliage growth rather than fruit. If you worry about lack of nutrients in your soil, a soil test can show what may be lacking. Harvest fruits continually as they ripen.

Saving Tomato Seeds

The beauty of saving tomato seeds resides in the timing. When your ripe tomatoes are ready to harvest, the seeds are ready for preserving too.

Tomato seeds are enclosed in a gelatinous sack, which contains chemicals that inhibit germination inside the tomato. In nature, a tomato falls off the vine, decomposes, and natural fermentation destroys the gel sac, allowing the seed to germinate in ideal conditions. To save tomato seeds, we simply mimic nature, fermenting the tomato seeds to remove the gel sac. It's a simple, if smelly, process, but fermentation also kills many seedborne tomato diseases. Here's how to do it.

↑ Tomato seeds are ready to harvest when the fruit is ripe for eating.

1 Wash the tomato, then slice it through the middle horizontally (not through the blossom end and core). This will expose the seed cavities.

> **.NOTE.**
>
>
>
> ───────────────
>
> If you're saving more than one variety of tomato seed, be certain to carefully clean your cutting board, knife, and strainer to avoid mixing seed varieties.

↑ Removing the seeds is easy—just squeeze.

2 Squeeze the seeds and surrounding gel into a bowl or canning jar. Label each container with the name of the tomato variety.

3 Add ½ cup (.12L) of water to the jar and stir it into the seed mixture. Let the mixture stand for 1–3 days, uncovered, at a temperature between 70–85°F.

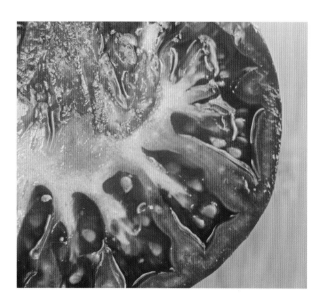

↑ Cut the tomato in slices horizontally to expose the seeds.

↑ Add water to the seeds and pulp. Stir well.

4 As the mixture ferments, white or grayish mold will appear on the surface. (Don't overferment, as seeds may begin to germinate.)

5 Add 1 cup (.24L) of water and stir the mix. Beware—it smells terrible. Let the mix rest. Viable seeds will settle to the bottom, while hollow seeds float to the top. Remove the floaters with a spoon.

6 Pour the mix through a fine-mesh strainer, rinsing with water until the seeds are clean from debris. Blot the excess water from the bottom of the strainer with a paper towel.

7 Pour the clean seeds from the strainer onto a plate. Spread the seeds into a single layer to dry. If you're working with more than one tomato variety at a time, label each plate with its variety.

8 Stir the seeds several times per day as they dry to ensure complete, even drying. Separate any clumps that form.

9 When seeds are completely dry (approximately one week), store them in an air-tight container in a cool, dry area, or freeze for long-term storage. Be certain to label your seeds carefully.

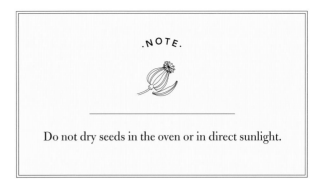

. N O T E .

Do not dry seeds in the oven or in direct sunlight.

↑ Pour the mix through a fine-mesh strainer, and rinse thoroughly.

↑ Fermenting is the worst part of the process—but it's necessary.

↑ Let the seeds dry well before storing.

SELECTING THE BEST TOMATOES FOR YOUR CLIMATE

Whether you grow in Northern climates with a short summer or in the Deep South where heat and humidity challenge your growing skills, the beauty of heirloom tomatoes lies in their heritage. Look for varieties that grow in climates similar to yours. For instance, tomatoes originating in Siberia work well for cooler climates with a short growing season. Tomatoes originating in Florida will withstand the hottest, longest seasons. Check the descriptions in seed catalogs to determine the best varieties for your garden.

Top 10 Heirloom Tomatoes for Cool, Short-Season Climates

- 'Alpha'
- 'Anna Russian'
- 'Buckbee's New 50-Day'
- 'Earliana'
- 'Galina'
- 'Glacier'
- 'Legend'
- 'Oregon Spring'
- 'Siberian'
- 'Stupice'

Top 10 Heirloom Tomatoes for Hot, Humid Climates

- 'Arkansas Traveler'
- 'Bali'
- 'Brandywine'
- 'Cherokee Purple'
- 'Costoluto Genovese'
- 'Floradade'
- 'Green Zebra'
- 'Homestead'
- 'Marglobe Supreme'
- 'Sioux'

← Make sure to note your favorite tomato varieties to grow again next year.

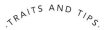

TOMATO

COMMON NAME: Tomato

SCIENTIFIC NAME: *Solanum lycopersicum*

FAMILY: Solanaceae

LIFE CYCLE: Short-lived perennial typically grown as an annual due to frost sensitivity.

FRUIT TYPE: Berry

SEED-STARTING DEPTH: ¼" (0.6 cm)

SEED-STARTING SOIL TEMPERATURE: 80°F (27°C). Bottom heat speeds germination.

SEED START TIMING: Start indoors 6–8 weeks prior to last frost.

LIGHT REQUIREMENTS: Not needed for germination. Direct light after germination, 1" (3 cm) above seedlings.

TRANSPLANT: Plant when two sets of true leaves appear. Transplant at least once to a larger container prior to planting out in garden.

DIRECT SOWING: Sow after danger of frost has passed.

GERMINATION: 4–8 days

DAYS TO MATURITY: 45–87. Fruit typically ripens 45–55 days after blossoming.

POLLINATION: Self

CROSS-POLLINATION: *Solanum lycopersicum* may cross pollinate with *Solanum pimpinellifolium* (currant tomato). Potato-leaf varieties may also cross-pollinate.

ISOLATION DISTANCE: 10–50' (3–15 m)

SEED MATURITY: Same as fruit ripeness/harvest maturity

SEED PROCESSING: Fermentation 1–3 days

SEED VIABILITY: 4–8 years

Eggplant
Solanum melongena, Solanum aethiopicum (Turkish Eggplant)

From the shiny, deep purple-black of 'Black Beauty' to the charming lavender-and-white striped 'Listada de Gandia' to the bright orange-and-green striped 'Turkish Orange', eggplants offer a rainbow of colors for the garden and dinner plate. Eggplants grow much like tomatoes. I recommend staking the plants because as the fruits grow and become heavy, they can topple the plant, causing breakage. Watch for pests that attack tomatoes, like hornworms, because they will also enjoy snacking on your eggplants.

I prefer harvesting eggplants while they're young and tender, before they become pithy. Use garden snips to harvest, as eggplants want to stay firmly attached to the plant. However, if you're saving seed, allow the eggplants to continue growing on the plant past market maturity. When they turn a yellowish brown and lose their shiny glow, it's time to harvest for seed. (They typically remove easily from the stem at this point as well.)

Eggplant seeds are firmly embedded in the fruit's flesh. It looks intimidating, but extracting the seeds is actually easy, if a tad messy. Cut the eggplant in half to make it easier to handle and use a hand grater to shred the flesh into a bowl. Fill the bowl with water until it covers the pulp and seeds by about 2 inches; agitate the water to separate the seeds from the pulp. The viable seeds will sink to the bottom of the bowl. Using a small strainer, scoop the floating debris from the top of the water, add more water, and repeat until the seeds look free of debris. Pour the water and seeds through a fine-mesh strainer, pat the bottom of the strainer with a paper towel to remove excess water, and pour seeds onto a paper plate to dry. Allow seeds to dry for about 2 weeks, stirring daily to ensure even drying. (Remember: process only one eggplant variety at a time to retain seed purity.)

EGGPLANT

COMMON NAMES: Eggplant, Aubergine/Turkish eggplant, Ethiopian eggplant

SCIENTIFIC NAMES: *Solanum melongena, Solanum aethiopicum*

FAMILY: Solanaceae

LIFE CYCLE: Tender perennial

FRUIT TYPE: Berry

SEED-STARTING DEPTH: ¼" (0.6 cm)

SPECIAL NEEDS: Bottom heat speeds germination.

SEED STARTING SOIL TEMPERATURE: 75–90°F (24–32°C)

SEED START TIMING: Start indoors using biodegradable containers 6–8 weeks before last frost. Bottom heat speeds germination.

LIGHT REQUIREMENTS: As soon as seedlings emerge

TRANSPLANT: Plant after danger of frost. Plant 18–24" (46–61 cm) apart. Stake taller varieties.

DIRECT SOWING: Not recommended

GERMINATION: 7–14 days

DAYS TO MATURITY: 100–150. Harvest eggplants young before their flesh becomes pithy.

POLLINATION: Self, insect

CROSS-POLLINATION: Can cross-pollinate with other varieties. Cage plants or bag blossoms to prevent cross-pollination. However, Turkish eggplant does not cross with garden eggplant varieties.

ISOLATION DISTANCE: 300–1,600' (91–488 m)

SEED MATURITY: After edible harvest. Fruit turns yellowish and dull when seeds ripen.

SEED PROCESSING: Wet process, rinse

SEED VIABILITY: 4–6 years

WANT TO ADD A RAINBOW TO YOUR GARDEN? GROW THESE EGGPLANTS

- White: 'Japanese White Egg'
- Yellow: 'Thai Yellow Egg'
- Light Green: 'Applegreen'
- Green Striped: 'Lao Green Stripe'
- Dark Green: 'Little Green'
- Orange: 'Turkish Orange'
- Red: 'Red China'
- Light Pink-Lavender: 'Rosa Bianca'
- Lavender: 'Rosita'
- Purple: 'Diamond'
- Purple-Black: 'Mitoyo'

Spinach
Spinacia oleracea

Spinach is one of my favorite vegetables, particularly when it's harvested young and sweet from the garden. It's a crop that's a little tricky though. Not only is it heat- and day-length sensitive, causing it to bolt and become bitter when its preferred cool growing days turn toasty and long, it's also a trickster when planning seed saving. Spinach is one of the few dioecious plants, which means that some plants are male, while others are female—and you won't know which it is until the plant flowers. Females are typically larger with slightly more pronounced flowers than the blooms on male plants. Make sure to cage plants in groups, using a cover of fine-spun polyester, to ensure adequate pollination (and to avoid cross-pollination from other varieties).

Spinach prefers nitrogen-rich soil and cool weather. This is a plant you can direct sow, even when the soil temperature is still chilly. In fact, spinach crops tolerate frost and freezes, still going strong when temperatures plunge to 15°F (-9°C). However, spinach is intolerant of heat and long days, causing it to bolt when day length reaches 13–15 hours. Additionally, for the best seed production, try to time the plants' flowers when temperatures are below 75°F (24°C). The good news? You can harvest some of the outer leaves of spinach plants, even if you intend to save seeds from the crop.

SPINACH

COMMON NAME: Spinach

SCIENTIFIC NAME: *Spinacia oleracea*

FAMILY: Chenopodiaceae

LIFE CYCLE: Annual

FRUIT TYPE: Dry indehiscent, single-seeded fruit (utricle)

SEED-STARTING DEPTH: ½" (1.3 cm)

SPECIAL NEEDS: Spinach requires cool temperatures to thrive.

SEED-STARTING SOIL TEMPERATURE: 40–75°F (4–24°C)

SEED START TIMING: Direct sow 3 weeks before last frost. Can be started indoors using biodegradable containers 4–5 weeks before last frost but does not transplant well, so plant containers directly in garden.

LIGHT REQUIREMENTS: As soon as seedlings emerge

TRANSPLANT: Plant 3 weeks prior to last frost. Do not disturb roots. Can tolerate temperatures to 15°F (-9°C).

DIRECT SOWING: Sow 3 weeks prior to last frost. Seeds can germinate in temperatures as low as 35°F (2°C). Seeds do not germinate well in soil temperatures above 75°F (24°C).

GERMINATION: 5–9 days

DAYS TO MATURITY: 40–52

POLLINATION: Wind. Plants are dioecious; some produce only male flowers, some only female. Spinach requires a 1:2 ratio male-to-female plants for best pollination. Cage several plants together for pollination.

CROSS-POLLINATION: Can cross-pollinate with other varieties. Cage plants using row cover fabric to prevent cross-pollination. Pollen is very fine, and isolation is the best method to ensure pure seed.

ISOLATION DISTANCE: 800'–1 mile (0.24–1.6 km)

SEED MATURITY: When plants turn yellow

SEED PROCESSING: Strip seeds by hand, winnow

SEED VIABILITY: 3 years

Corn
Zea mays

Growing up on a dairy farm after the Great Depression, my dad never glamorized farm life. In fact, he was quick to leave the manure spreader behind and head off to college. While my dad may have left the farm, he never lost his farm-boy love of sweet corn. Every summer Saturday, we drove around the Indiana countryside, looking for fresh-from-the-field sweet corn. And I mean fresh. If the corn was harvested more than an hour or two before we arrived at the farm stand, forget it—my dad considered it old.

Today I'm the keeper of that sweet corn tradition. Growing sweet corn is an homage to my dad, plus it guarantees that we only eat the sweetest, freshest ears. Growing corn—whether it's sweet, flint, flour, dent, or popcorn—can be a challenge for the home gardener, particularly if you want to save seeds. Corn is a real-estate intensive crop; you need a fairly large garden to grow enough corn to ensure genetic diversity. Corn is a crop that suffers from inbreeding depression, which if not addressed, will lead to disappointing future harvests from saved seeds.

For the best pollination and seed set, plant corn in blocks six rows wide, with plants spaced 6–12 inches (15–30 cm) apart and 24–36 inches (61–91 cm) between rows. Corn is monecious, meaning that separate male and female flowers are produced on each plant. Male flowers, the tassels on top of the corn stalk, pollinate the female flowers, the tiny hairs on the silks, by wind. The corncob is the ovary receptacle, and the ovaries eventually become the kernels of the corn. Tasseling occurs about 3 weeks after pollination. Hand-pollination is recommended to improve pollination.

·TRAITS AND TIPS·

CORN

COMMON NAMES: Corn, sweet corn, flint corn, popcorn, dent corn, maize

SCIENTIFIC NAME: *Zea mays*

FAMILY: Poacea

LIFE CYCLE: Annual

FRUIT TYPE: Dry indehiscent, single-seeded (caryopses)

SEED-STARTING DEPTH: 1½" (3.8 cm)

SPECIAL NEEDS: Plant in blocks of six rows for best pollination.

SEED-STARTING SOIL TEMPERATURE: 60–95°F (16–35°C)

SEED START TIMING: Direct sowing after frost is preferred. Can be started indoors using biodegradable containers 4 weeks before last frost. Bottom heat speeds germination.

LIGHT REQUIREMENTS: As soon as seedlings emerge

TRANSPLANT: Plant after danger of frost. Do not disturb roots. Plant in blocks of six rows for best pollination and kernel set. Space plants 6–12" (15–30 cm) apart, 24–36" (61–91 cm) between rows.

DIRECT SOWING: Sow after danger of frost has passed and when temperatures reach 50°F (10°C).

GERMINATION: 5–14 days

DAYS TO MATURITY: 60–100, depending on variety

POLLINATION: Wind

CROSS-POLLINATION: Can cross-pollinate with other varieties. Bag shoots and tassels and hand-pollinate. (See sidebar.)

ISOLATION DISTANCE: 800'–½ mile (0.24–0.8 km)

SEED MATURITY: Dry on plant. Seeds reach maturity when husks are dry and brown and kernels are hard.

SEED PROCESSING: Hand; twist ears to remove kernels.

SEED VIABILITY: 2–3 years

HOW TO HAND-POLLINATE CORN

- As tassels emerge, look for the shoots on a stalk. Cover the shoots with bags before the silk emerges.

- Remove husk leaves, which grow along the stem and encase the silk and tiny ears of corn. Cut the main leaf next to a shoot to secure the bag over the shoot. Close the bottom of the bag securely with staples or binder clips.

- Place another bag over the tassels. Fasten the bottom of the bag securely. (The anthers will shed pollen into the bag.)

- The same day as you cover the tassels, cut the tip of the shoot's husk to expose the silks. Replace the bag.

- Remove the tassel bag carefully, making sure not to spill the pollen. Remove the shoot bag and sprinkle pollen onto the silks of the shoot, which will have emerged past the cut shoot tip.

- Immediately after pollination, cover the shoot with a bag to prevent any cross-contamination. Secure the bag. Mark the shoot for seed saving.

- Remove the bag when the silks are dry and kernels begin forming.

- Let the corn ears mature and dry on plant.

- Harvest the corn for seed saving approximately 4 to 6 weeks after market maturity.

- Pull back the corn husk to expose the seed and hang to dry fully.

- Harvest seeds by rubbing kernels to release seeds over a container.

CHAPTER 5

Herbs and Flowers

Congratulations! You now know how to grow your own food from seed, and how to save seed from your crops. You're ready to go off-grid and live a self-sustainable life. Or at least, you'll grow some darn fine tomatoes to share with friends and family.

But seed starting and saving isn't just for growing vegetables and fruit. While many gardeners incorporate flowers and herbs into the kitchen garden, some gardeners prefer to focus on ornamentals, or may only grow herbs to enhance their culinary interests. Growing both flowers and herbs from seeds is easy and saving seeds from your garden is a perfect way to save money while benefitting pollinators— and your taste buds. This chapter introduces you to some of the best herbs and flowers for your garden, all organized alphabetically by their Latin names.

Herbs

Some of the loveliest flowers used to attract pollinators or add to bouquets are classified as herbs. Not only do herbs provide beauty in the garden, many create a culinary masterpiece from a plain piece of meat, while others have been used as medicinal remedies throughout history.

Let's pause for a moment while I add an important disclaimer: *Please consult a professional before using herbs for medical purposes.* I am a gardener, not a medical professional. Please be careful when treating ailments with herbs.

Yarrow
Achillea millefoliu

Along with its traditional healing properties, yarrow is also used as a flavoring for beer, wine, and soft drinks. Personally, though, I prefer to enjoy yarrow in the garden. It's a pollinator magnet, attracting beneficial insects, such as brachnoid wasps, that prey on garden pests. Plus, deer and rabbits will avoid eating it, as they dislike the ferny texture.

YARROW

COMMON NAME: Yarrow

SCIENTIFIC NAME: *Achillea millefolium*

FAMILY: Asteraceae

LIFE CYCLE: Perennial

USES: Cut flower, landscape, borders, cottage garden, pollinators, companion plant, medicinal.

FRUIT TYPE: Achenes

SEED-STARTING DEPTH: Surface sow

SPECIAL NEEDS: Needs light to germinate. Bottom heat speeds germination. Some varieties benefit from stratification.

SEED-STARTING SOIL TEMPERATURE: 65–75°F (18–24°C)

SEED START TIMING: Start seeds indoors 8–10 weeks prior to last frost using biodegradable containers.

LIGHT REQUIREMENTS: It needs light to germinate. As seedlings emerge, continue 12–16 hours of light per day.

TRANSPLANT: Plant after danger of frost, in full sun. Tolerates poor soil as long as it's well drained. Space plants 12" (30 cm) apart.

DIRECT SOWING: Sow after danger of frost has passed and when soil temperature reaches 55°F (13°C). Can sow in late fall in mild climates. May also be winter sown.

GERMINATION: 10–14 days

DAYS TO MATURITY: 120–130

POLLINATION: Insect

CROSS-POLLINATION: Can cross-pollinate with other varieties. Cage plants or bag blossoms to prevent cross-pollination.

ISOLATION DISTANCE: ¼ mile (0.4 km)

SEED MATURITY: Dry flower heads on the plants and hand harvest or harvest whole stems prior to frost. Bundle stems and hang upside down to dry thoroughly.

SEED PROCESSING: Remove flower heads and spread them out to dry on a screen. Thresh or rub the flower heads to release seed. Winnow to remove debris.

SEED VIABILITY: 5 years

Chive
Allium schoenoprasum,
Allium tuberosum

Historically, clusters of chives were hung in homes to drive away diseases and evil. Today, chives add a tasty kick to culinary dishes, while also offering beautiful blooms that attract pollinators. But guess what? Humans find the blooms tasty too. The edible flowers add zip as a pretty, delicious garnish.

↑ Chive blossoms add a tasty garnish to meals.

CHIVE

COMMON NAME: Chive

SCIENTIFIC NAME: *Allium schoenoprasum* (common chives), *Allium tuberosum* (Chinese chives, garlic chives)

FAMILY: Amaryllidaceae

LIFE CYCLE: Perennial

USES: Culinary, landscape, borders, containers, pollinators, edible flowers, medicinal

FRUIT TYPE: Dehiscent capsule

SEED-STARTING DEPTH: ¼" (0.6 cm)

SPECIAL NEEDS: Plants require exposure to temperatures 40–55°F (4–13°C) for 4–8 weeks before flowering and setting viable seed. May flower in its first year, but seeds will not be viable until its second year.

SEED-STARTING SOIL TEMPERATURE: 68–75°F (20–24°C)

SEED START TIMING: Direct sow after frost. Can be started indoors using biodegradable containers 8–10 weeks before last frost. Bottom heat speeds germination.

LIGHT REQUIREMENTS: As soon as seedlings emerge.

TRANSPLANT: Plant in full sun after danger of frost. Do not disturb roots. Space 4–6" (8–15 cm) apart. Prefers moist, rich, well-drained soil. Divide plants every 3–4 years to keep them productive.

DIRECT SOWING: Sow after danger of frost has passed when soil temperature reaches 55°F (13°C).

GERMINATION: 10–21 days

DAYS TO MATURITY: 60–70

POLLINATION: Insect

CROSS-POLLINATION: Can cross-pollinate with other varieties. Cage plants or bag blossoms to prevent cross-pollination.

ISOLATION DISTANCE: 800'–½ mile (0.24–0.8 km)

SEED MATURITY: Capsules split open to expose mature seeds. Harvest flower heads and spread on screens to dry completely.

SEED PROCESSING: Rub, thresh

SEED VIABILITY: 2 years

Dill
Anethum graveolens

A natural companion for pickling cucumbers, dill is also the host plant to swallowtail butterfly larvae. One of my proudest gardening moments involved my youngest son—and a farm tour. Several years ago, the Carolina Farm Stewardship Association asked to include our gardens on their South Carolina farm tour so people could see the possibility of growing food in their own yards. Hundreds of guests visited our garden, and we met lovely people. While touring the property, an older fellow looked at one of my (many) patches of dill and proclaimed loudly, "You'd better get the spray out. You've got worms all over your dill." My son, then about seven years old, said (equally loudly), "Don't you know that we're organic? That dill feeds swallowtail caterpillars!"

It was a little cheeky, but the lesson here is: Kids pay attention. Plant lots of dill. Cover some of the plants with row cover cloth to preserve it for your use, but also—share some with wildlife. You'll be happy you did when your garden is filled with butterflies.

DILL

COMMON NAME: Dill

SCIENTIFIC NAME: *Anethum graveolens*

FAMILY: Apiaceae

LIFE CYCLE: Annual

USES: Culinary, landscape, container, pollinators, companion plant. Attracts beneficial insects.

FRUIT TYPE: Schizocarp splits at maturity into two, single-seeded mericarps.

SEED-STARTING DEPTH: ¼" (0.6 cm)

SPECIAL NEEDS: Plant extra dill as it serves as a host plant for swallowtail butterfly larvae. Succession planting throughout summer ensures continuous supply.

SEED-STARTING SOIL TEMPERATURE: 60–70°F (16–21°C)

SEED START TIMING: Direct sowing after frost is preferred. Can be started indoors using biodegradable containers 6–8 weeks before last frost. Bottom heat speeds germination.

LIGHT REQUIREMENTS: As soon as seedlings emerge

TRANSPLANT: Plant in full sun after danger of frost has passed. Do not disturb roots. Space 4" apart.

DIRECT SOWING: Sow after danger of frost has passed when soil temperature reaches 60°F (16°C).

GERMINATION: 7–21 days

DAYS TO MATURITY: 50–60 for leaf harvest; 85–105 for seed harvest

POLLINATION: Insect

CROSS-POLLINATION: Can cross-pollinate with other varieties. Cage plants or bag blossoms to prevent cross-pollination.

ISOLATION DISTANCE: 800' (0.24 km)

SEED MATURITY: Seeds are mature when the flower head is dry and brown. Hand harvest carefully. Shattering is common.

SEED PROCESSING: Thresh

SEED VIABILITY: 5 years

Chervil
Anthriscus cerefolium

If you're a foodie, chervil deserves a place in your garden. Chervil roots historically were thought to prevent plague and cure hiccups. So, not only can you serve friends a delicious, herb-infused meal, you can send them home with a tonic to keep them plague-free. How thoughtful.

CHEVRIL

COMMON NAME: Chervil, garden chervil, french parsley

SCIENTIFIC NAME: *Anthriscus cerefolium*

FAMILY: Apiaceae

LIFE CYCLE: Annual

USES: Culinary, medicinal, companion plant, borders, containers, pollinators

FRUIT TYPE: Schizocarps

SEED-STARTING DEPTH: Surface sow

SPECIAL NEEDS: Soak seeds overnight prior to planting. Needs light for germination. Plants will bolt in hot weather; it prefers cooler temperatures.

SEED-STARTING SOIL TEMPERATURE: 60–70°F (16–21°C)

SEED START TIMING: Start indoors using biodegradable containers 4–6 weeks before last frost.

LIGHT REQUIREMENTS: It needs light to germinate. As seedlings emerge, continue 12–16 hours of light per day.

TRANSPLANT: Plant in full or part sun after danger of frost has passed. Do not disturb roots. Plant in deep beds, as chervil grows long taproots. Space 6–10" (15–25 cm) apart.

DIRECT SOWING: Sow 2 to 3 weeks before last frost.

GERMINATION: 14–28 days

DAYS TO MATURITY: 60–65

POLLINATION: Insect

CROSS-POLLINATION: Can cross-pollinate with other varieties. Cage plants or bag blossoms to prevent cross-pollination.

ISOLATION DISTANCE: ¼ mile (0.4 km)

SEED MATURITY: Dry flower heads on plants or harvest prior to frost and allow seedheads to continue to dry fully. Spread out to dry.

SEED PROCESSING: Thresh

SEED VIABILITY: 1 year

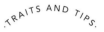

BORAGE

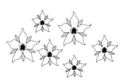

SCIENTIFIC NAME: *Borago officinalis*

FAMILY: Boraginaceae

LIFE CYCLE: Annual

USES: Culinary, companion plant, medicinal, containers, pollinators, edible flowers and leaves

FRUIT TYPE: Nutlet

SEED-STARTING DEPTH: ¼" (0.6 cm)

SPECIAL NEEDS: Grow in the dark until it germinates.

SEED-STARTING SOIL TEMPERATURE: 65–85°F (18–29°C)

Borage
Borago officinalis

We celebrate borage for its cucumber-flavored edible leaves and flowers, as well as for its companionable ability to enhance the flavors of vegetables planted near it. Pollinators adore its brilliant, star-shaped flowers while pests prefer to stay away. Tasty, beautiful, and a natural pollinator magnet; if only all plants worked so hard! Harvest young, tender leaves 6–8 weeks after planting and use them fresh. Don't freeze, as borage loses flavor.

SEED START TIMING: Direct sowing after frost is preferred. Can be started indoors using biodegradable containers 6–8 weeks before last frost. Bottom heat speeds germination.

LIGHT REQUIREMENTS: As soon as seedlings emerge

TRANSPLANT: Plant in full or part sun after danger of frost has passed. Do not disturb roots. Space 12" (30 cm) apart. Prefers rich, well-drained soil. Readily self-sows and may become weedy.

DIRECT SOWING: Sow after danger of frost has passed, when soil temperatures reach 60°F (16°C).

GERMINATION: 7–14 days

DAYS TO MATURITY: 50 to 60

POLLINATION: Insect

CROSS-POLLINATION: Can cross-pollinate with other varieties. Cage plants or bag blossoms to prevent cross-pollination.

ISOLATION DISTANCE: ¼ mile (0.4 km)

SEED MATURITY: Harvest when flowers fade and turn brown. Harvest dried flower heads by hand.

SEED PROCESSING: Thresh or rub to remove seeds; winnow.

SEED VIABILITY: 3–5 years

Calendula
Calendula officinalis

While known to symbolize sorrow or sympathy in the language of flowers, calendula's bright, cheerful blooms represent anything but sadness. Its distinct odor discourages pests and repels mosquitos, making it a perfect plant for entranceways or patios. Often referred to as "poor man's saffron," calendula substituted for the expensive spice adds color and flavor to culinary creations. While both its flowers and leaves are edible, the leaves aren't tasty. They're rather bitter, in fact. Stick to the beautiful blooms for dining pleasures but enjoy the entire plant in your garden.

CALENDULA

COMMON NAMES: Calendula, pot marigold, English marigold

SCIENTIFIC NAME: *Calendula officinalis*

FAMILY: Asteraceae

LIFE CYCLE: Annual

USES: Culinary, medicinal, companion plant, landscape, cottage garden, cut flowers, containers, edible flower (only eat petals, not calyx or flower centers)

FRUIT TYPE: Achenes

SEED-STARTING DEPTH: ¼" (0.6 cm)

SPECIAL NEEDS: It needs dark to germinate.

SEED-STARTING SOIL TEMPERATURE: 68–70°F (20–21°C)

SEED START TIMING: Direct sow after frost. Can be started indoors using biodegradable containers 6–8 weeks before last frost.

LIGHT REQUIREMENTS: As seedlings emerge, place under lights for 12–16 hours per day.

TRANSPLANT: Plant in full sun after danger of frost has passed. Do not disturb roots. Space 6–12" (15–30 cm) apart for smaller varieties, 18–24" (46–61 cm) apart for tall varieties.

DIRECT SOWING: Sow after danger of frost has passed and when soil temperature reaches 60°F (16°C).

GERMINATION: 14–21 days

DAYS TO MATURITY: 60–70

POLLINATION: Insect

CROSS-POLLINATION: Can cross-pollinate with other varieties. Cage plants or bag blossoms to prevent cross-pollination.

ISOLATION DISTANCE: ⅛ mile (0.2 km)

SEED MATURITY: Harvest flowers as they begin to fade. Seed continues to ripen as the flower dries. Spread flower heads in a warm, dry place until dry.

SEED PROCESSING: Rub and flail to release seeds. Dry seeds 1 week before storing.

SEED VIABILITY: 9 years

Chamomile
Chamaemelum nobile,
Matricaria recutita

Confusion often arises about the varieties of chamomile. Roman chamomile, a perennial, was formerly known as *Anthemis nobile* but renamed as *Chamaemelum nobile.* Roman chamomile is shorter and a good variety for planting between pavers or as a border. German chamomile, *Matricaria recutita,* is grown as an annual. German chamomile is taller and blooms more prolifically than Roman chamomile, but both have similar cheerful, small, daisylike flowers with hints of apple fragrance. You can harvest both varieties of chamomile, drying the flower heads, and using them for your own bedtime tea. (Note: if you're allergic to ragweed, there's a possibility you may be allergic to chamomile. Please discuss with your doctor prior to consuming chamomile in any way!)

CHAMOMILE

COMMON NAMES: Roman chamomile, German chamomile

SCIENTIFIC NAME: *Chamaemelum nobile* (Roman), *Matricaria recutita* (German)

FAMILY: Asteraceae

LIFE CYCLE: Perennial (Roman), Annual (German)

USES: Culinary, medicinal, cut flowers, landscape, containers, pollinators, borders

FRUIT TYPE: Achenes

SEED-STARTING DEPTH: ¼" (0.6 cm)

SPECIAL NEEDS: It needs light to germinate.

SEED-STARTING SOIL TEMPERATURE: 68–70°F (20–21°C)

SEED START TIMING: Direct sow after frost. Can be started indoors using biodegradable containers 6–8 weeks before last frost.

LIGHT REQUIREMENTS: It needs light to germinate. As seedlings emerge, continue 12–16 hours of light per day.

TRANSPLANT: Plant in full or part sun after danger of frost. Needs well-drained soil. Roman chamomile grows low and spreads. Space 8" (20 cm) apart for Roman varieties, 10" (25 cm) apart for German.

DIRECT SOWING: Sow after danger of frost has passed and when temperatures reach 60°F (16 C).

GERMINATION: 14–21 days

DAYS TO MATURITY: 60–65

POLLINATION: Insect

CROSS-POLLINATION: Can cross-pollinate with other varieties. Cage plants or bag blossoms to prevent cross-pollination.

ISOLATION DISTANCE: ½ mile (0.8 km)

SEED MATURITY: Dry flowers on plants or harvest spent blooms prior to frost and continue to dry fully. Collect dried heads by hand.

SEED PROCESSING: Rub, thresh, or flail

SEED VIABILITY: 3 years

Cilantro/Coriander
Coriandrum sativum

Do you love cilantro or do you think it tastes like soap? Interestingly, our genes determine whether we enjoy the flavor of this herb or are repulsed by it. Cilantro and coriander confuse some gardeners. When grown for its seeds, this herb is known as coriander. When grown for leaves, this plant is known as cilantro. Regardless, the plant doesn't tolerate heat well and prefers cool temperatures. Excessive heat leads to bolting . . . turning your cilantro into coriander, which really isn't a tragedy.

CILANTRO/CORIANDER

COMMON NAMES: Cilantro/coriander, Chinese parsley

SCIENTIFIC NAME: *Coriandrum sativum*

FAMILY: Apiaceae

LIFE CYCLE: Annual

USES: Culinary, medicinal, companion plant, containers, borders

FRUIT TYPE: Schizocarp

SEED-STARTING DEPTH: ¼–½" (0.6–1.3 cm)

SPECIAL NEEDS: Soak seeds in water overnight prior to planting. It needs darkness to germinate.

SEED-STARTING SOIL TEMPERATURE: 55–68°F (13–20°C)

SEED START TIMING: Direct sowing after frost is preferred. Can be started indoors using biodegradable containers 4–5 weeks before last frost.

LIGHT REQUIREMENTS: As soon as seedlings emerge

TRANSPLANT: Plant in full sun or part shade after danger of frost has passed. Do not disturb roots. Space plants 2–4" (5–10 cm) apart for leaf crop, 8" (20 cm) apart to grow for seed. Cilantro grows well even in crowded conditions.

DIRECT SOWING: Sow after danger of frost has passed and when temperatures reach 55°F (13°C).

GERMINATION: 14–21 days

DAYS TO MATURITY: 60–70 days for leaves, 100-plus days for seed

POLLINATION: Insect

CROSS-POLLINATION: Can cross-pollinate, but as there aren't many varieties—not a big concern. Cage plants or bag blossoms to prevent cross-pollination.

ISOLATION DISTANCE: ½ mile (0.8 km)

SEED MATURITY: Approximately 2–3 weeks after flowering. Dry flower umbels on the plants or harvest prior to frost and continue to dry. Place flower heads in bags and hang upside down to catch seed as it dries.

SEED PROCESSING: Rub, thresh

SEED VIABILITY: 2–4 years

Lemongrass
Cymbopogon citratus

If you typically plant ornamental grass in your landscape, it's time to consider adding lemongrass in its place. Not only does the plant produce a lovely citrus scent that helps repel mosquitoes, it can be harvested and used dried, fresh, or in powder form. Popular for Asian dishes, lemongrass also makes a delicious ingredient for tea. Best of all, though, by planting lemongrass in your landscape, you'll enjoy gorgeous autumn color as its leaves change from summer green to fiery red. Plant several clusters so you'll have plenty of lemongrass both for your pantry and your landscape. (Warning: wear gloves when harvesting or dividing plants. Lemongrass blades are sharp.)

SEED START TIMING: Start indoors using biodegradable containers 6–8 weeks before last frost.

LIGHT REQUIREMENTS: As soon as seedlings emerge

TRANSPLANT: Plant in full or part sun after danger of frost, when nighttime temperatures reach 50°F (10°C). Do not disturb roots. Space 8–12" (20–30 cm) apart. Prefers moist, rich, loamy soil. Keep well watered.

DIRECT SOWING: Sow after danger of frost has passed and when soil temperatures reach 50°F (10°C).

GERMINATION: 5–21 days

DAYS TO MATURITY: 75–85

POLLINATION: Wind

CROSS-POLLINATION: Can cross-pollinate with other varieties. Cage plants or bag blossoms to prevent cross-pollination.

ISOLATION DISTANCE: ¼ mile (0.4 km)

SEED MATURITY: Dry seedheads on plants or harvest prior to frost and allow the pods to continue to dry fully.

SEED PROCESSING: Thresh

SEED VIABILITY: 1 year (Note: fresh seed does not germinate well. Store seed for 2 months before sowing.)

LEMONGRASS

COMMON NAME: Lemongrass

SCIENTIFIC NAME: *Cymbopogon citratus*

FAMILY: Poaceae

LIFE CYCLE: Tender perennial

USES: Culinary, medicinal, landscape, companion plant, containers

FRUIT TYPE: Caryopsis

SEED-STARTING DEPTH: ¼" (0.6 cm)

SPECIAL NEEDS: It needs dark for germination. Keep seed mix moist, not wet.

SEED-STARTING SOIL TEMPERATURE: 70–85°F (21–29°C)

Coneflower
Echinacea spp.

If you add only one flowering herb to your garden, grow *Echinacea*. From the most common purple coneflowers (*E. purpurea*) to the yellow *E. paradoxa*, the blooms of echinacea attract pollinators and add beauty to your garden. Echinacea's immune boosting reputation makes the plant popular among herbalists. Growing coneflower from seed isn't difficult, but different varieties require different seed-starting procedures, listed below. When harvesting seeds, leave a few seedheads on the plants, and you'll encourage birds to visit your garden for snacks.

CONEFLOWER

COMMON NAMES: Coneflower, purple coneflower, Eastern purple coneflower

SCIENTIFIC NAMES: *Echinacea* spp., including *E. tennesseensis, E. paradoxa, E. angustifolia, E. pallida, E. purpurea* (common purple coneflower)

FAMILY: Asteraceae

LIFE CYCLE: Perennial

USES: Cut flower, medicinal, landscape, containers, pollinators, companion plant, dried flower

FRUIT TYPE: Achenes

SEED-STARTING DEPTH: ⅛" (0.3 cm)

SPECIAL NEEDS: It needs dark for germination. *E. angustifolia, E. paradoxa,* and *E. tennesseensis* require stratification. Sow seeds at 68°F (20°C) for a month, move to 41°F (5°C) for 10 weeks, then germinate at 50°F (10°C).

SEED-STARTING SOIL TEMPERATURE: 65–70°F (18–21°C)

SEED START TIMING: Start indoors using biodegradable containers 8–10 weeks before last frost. Can winter sow. (See notes for varieties requiring stratification.)

LIGHT REQUIREMENTS: As soon as seedlings emerge

TRANSPLANT: Plant in full sun or part shade in well-drained soil after danger of frost. Space 12" (30 cm) apart.

DIRECT SOWING: Sow after danger of frost has passed and when soil temperatures reach 65°F (18°C). Can plant in fall for natural stratification.

GERMINATION: 20–30 days, depending on variety

DAYS TO MATURITY: 300–365 (blooms second year)

POLLINATION: Insect

CROSS-POLLINATION: Can cross-pollinate with other varieties. Cage plants or bag blossoms to prevent cross-pollination.

ISOLATION DISTANCE: ½ mile (0.8 km)

SEED MATURITY: Seeds mature when flowers fade and dry. Dry flowers on plants or harvest prior to frost and allow seedheads to continue to dry fully.

SEED PROCESSING: Thresh. Wear gloves if separating seeds by hand.

SEED VIABILITY: 3 years

Fennel
Foeniculum vulgare

If you adore beneficial insects and fabulous texture in the garden, as well as tasty culinary treats, fennel is your plant. Choose between two types: Fennel harvested for its bulb, like Florence fennel, and fennel harvested for leaves, such as bronze fennel. Or even better, grow them both! Fennel offers delicious flavor and fabulous foliage, plus when it's allowed to flower, it's an excellent companion plant to attract beneficial insects to the garden.

·TRAITS AND TIPS·

FENNEL

COMMON NAMES: Fennel, Florence fennel, finocchio, sweet fennel, bronze fennel

SCIENTIFIC NAME: *Foeniculum vulgare*

FAMILY: Apiaceae

LIFE CYCLE: Perennial, Biennial, Annual (Florence fennel: annual for food, biennial for seed; Sweet fennel: perennial)

USES: Culinary, medicinal, companion plant, pollinators, cut flower, foliage

FRUIT TYPE: Schizocarp

SEED-STARTING DEPTH: ½" (1.3 cm)

SPECIAL NEEDS: None

SEED-STARTING SOIL TEMPERATURE: 50–75°F (10–24°C)

SEED START TIMING: Direct sowing after frost is preferred. Can be started indoors using biodegradable containers 4–6 weeks before last frost. Time sowing to harvest bulbs in cooler weather, or plants may bolt in the heat.

LIGHT REQUIREMENTS: As soon as seedlings emerge

TRANSPLANT: Plant in full sun after danger of frost. Do not disturb roots. Space 6" (15 cm) apart. Plants require steady moisture to produce bulbs.

DIRECT SOWING: Sow after danger of frost has passed and when temperatures reach 55°F (13°C).

GERMINATION: 7–14 days

DAYS TO MATURITY: 50–80, depending on variety. Seeds are produced the second year after flowering.

POLLINATION: Insect

CROSS-POLLINATION: Can cross-pollinate with other varieties. Cage plants or bag blossoms to prevent cross-pollination.

ISOLATION DISTANCE: ½ mile (0.8 km)

SEED MATURITY: Select seeds from late-bolting plants. Harvest umbels as they begin to brown.

SEED PROCESSING: Flail, hand. Cure seeds 4–5 days in warm, dry location prior to storing.

SEED VIABILITY: 4 years

Roselle
Hibiscus sabdariffa

One of the prettiest and easiest plants to grow from seed, roselle, a relative of cotton and okra, forms beautiful blooms while offering flamboyant red calyces that are good enough to eat. In fact, it's best known for its use in Red Zinger tea. I overwinter my roselle in a large container in an unheated greenhouse, and it comes back nicely each year. In colder climates, treat it as an annual. Roselle grows 5–7 feet (1.5–2.1 m) and adds a tropical feel to any patio or pool.

ROSELLE

COMMON NAMES: Roselle, Florida cranberry, red sorrel, Jamaica sorrel

SCIENTIFIC NAME: *Hibiscus sabdariffa*

FAMILY: Malvaceae

LIFE CYCLE: Tender perennial

USES: Culinary, medicinal, containers, landscape, pollinators, ornamental

FRUIT TYPE: Capsule

SEED-STARTING DEPTH: ½" (1.3 cm)

SPECIAL NEEDS: Scarify seeds prior to planting.

SEED-STARTING SOIL TEMPERATURE: 75–85°F (24–29°C)

SEED START TIMING: Start indoors using biodegradable containers 6–8 weeks before last frost. Bottom heat speeds germination.

LIGHT REQUIREMENTS: As soon as seedlings emerge

TRANSPLANT: Plant in full sun in well-drained soil after danger of frost. Do not disturb roots. Space 36" (91 cm) apart. Grows well in large containers.

DIRECT SOWING: Sow after danger of frost has passed and when temperatures reach 55°F (13°C).

GERMINATION: 7–14 days

DAYS TO MATURITY: 90–100. Harvest at 90–150 days. Roselle begins producing flowers as daylight shortens.

POLLINATION: Insect

CROSS-POLLINATION: Can cross-pollinate with other varieties, but research shows low rate of cross-pollination. Cage plants or bag blossoms as a preventative.

ISOLATION DISTANCE: ¼ mile (0.4 km)

SEED MATURITY: Dry calyxes on plants or harvest prior to frost and allow to continue to dry fully. Brownish pods indicate seeds are mature. Peel off petals, remove seeds from the calyx, and dry fully before storing.

SEED PROCESSING: Thresh

SEED VIABILITY: 2–3 years

St. John's Wort
Hypericum perforatum

From association with the sun god Baldor to its ties to St. John to its historical use to ward off evil spirits and thunderbolts, St. John's wort offers an interesting history. While herbalists use the herb to treat mild depression, its stunning display of cheerful yellow blooms alone can cheer gloomy moods. Plus, pollinators swarm St. John's wort when it's in bloom. Consider planting it near your vegetable garden to encourage pollination.

ST. JOHN'S WORT

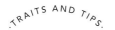

COMMON NAME: St. John's wort

SCIENTIFIC NAME: *Hypericum perforatum*

FAMILY: Hypericaceae

LIFE CYCLE: Short-lived perennial

USES: Medicinal, landscape, pollinators, containers

FRUIT TYPE: Capsule

SEED-STARTING DEPTH: ¼" (0.6 cm)

SPECIAL NEEDS: Stratify 3–4 weeks to improve germination. It needs light to germinate.

SEED-STARTING SOIL TEMPERATURE: 60–75°F (16–24°C)

SEED START TIMING: Start indoors using biodegradable containers 6–8 weeks before last frost. Bottom heat speeds germination.

LIGHT REQUIREMENTS: It needs light to germinate. As seedlings emerge, continue 12–16 hours of light per day.

TRANSPLANT: Plant in full sun or part shade in well-drained soil after danger of frost. Do not disturb roots, as it grows long taproots. Space plants 18–24" (46–61 cm) apart.

DIRECT SOWING: Sow after danger of frost has passed and when temperatures reach 55°F (13°C). Can sow in autumn for natural stratification.

GERMINATION: 10–14 days

DAYS TO MATURITY: 90–120. Most varieties flower their second year.

POLLINATION: Self, insect

CROSS-POLLINATION: Can cross-pollinate with other varieties. Cage plants or bag blossoms to prevent cross-pollination.

ISOLATION DISTANCE: ½ mile (0.8 km)

SEED MATURITY: Seeds mature after plants flower the second year. Gather seeds from ripe capsules. Capsules turn reddish brown as they mature.

SEED PROCESSING: Thresh

SEED VIABILITY: 5–7 years; allow a period of seed dormancy prior to germinating.

Lavender
Lavandula spp.

When planning an herb garden, lavender is often one of the first additions. Its delicate blooms and sweet fragrance makes a lovely addition to borders along walkways, where you can enjoy the scent, as well as a companion plant near vegetable gardens to encourage pollinators, as bees adore the blooms. However, lavender is a tad finicky. Be certain to plant lavender in full sun in well-drained, fairly dry soil, and keep it out of standing water, or you'll lose your plant to root rot.

SEED-STARTING SOIL TEMPERATURE: 70–80°F (21–27°C)

SEED START TIMING: Start indoors using biodegradable containers 10–12 weeks before last frost. Bottom heat speeds germination.

LIGHT REQUIREMENTS: It needs light to germinate. As seedlings emerge, continue 12–16 hours of light per day.

TRANSPLANT: Plant in full sun in well-drained soil after danger of frost. Space 12–15" (30–38 cm) apart. Lavender will not tolerate wet feet.

DIRECT SOWING: Not recommended

GERMINATION: 14–21 days

DAYS TO MATURITY: 90–200, depending on variety

POLLINATION: Insect

CROSS-POLLINATION: Can cross-pollinate with other varieties. Cage plants or bag blossoms to prevent cross-pollination.

ISOLATION DISTANCE: ½ mile (0.8 km)

SEED MATURITY: Allow flowers to dry on plants. Snip the stems, bundle, place a paper bag over the flower heads, and hang upside down until completely dry. Harvest seeds when they're brown and dry.

SEED PROCESSING: Thresh

SEED VIABILITY: 2 years

·TRAITS AND TIPS·

LAVENDER

COMMON NAME: Lavender

SCIENTIFIC NAMES: *Lavandula* spp. *L. augustifolia* (English), *L. intermedia* (Provence), *L. stoechas* (Spanish), *L. dentata* (French)

FAMILY: Lamiaceae

LIFE CYCLE: Perennial

USES: Culinary, medicinal, aromatherapy, perfume, edible flowers, pollinators, companion plant, hedge, landscape, cut flower

FRUIT TYPE: Nutlet

SEED-STARTING DEPTH: ⅛" (0.3 cm)

SPECIAL NEEDS: It needs light to germinate. Cold stratify 4 weeks to boost germination. Use very light seed-starting mix or vermiculite that drains quickly for germination. Bottom heat speeds germination. Note: Lavender is susceptible to damping off. Keep soil moist but not wet and provide good air circulation.

Lemon Balm
Melissa officinalis

Called the "Elixir of Life," lemon balm provides an amazing burst of aromatherapy when working next to it in the garden. I often pull a few sprigs to sniff when I need a mood or energy boost. Delicious when used in tea, lemon balm imparts calming properties. However, as a member of the mint family, lemon balm spreads rapidly. Consider growing it in a container to avoid it spreading invasively throughout the garden.

SEED-STARTING SOIL TEMPERATURE: 68–70°F (20–21°C)

SEED START TIMING: Start indoors using biodegradable containers 6–8 weeks before last frost.

LIGHT REQUIREMENTS: It needs light to germinate. As seedlings emerge, continue 12–16 hours of light per day.

TRANSPLANT: Plant in full sun to part shade in well-drained soil after danger of frost. Space 12" (30 cm) apart. Plants spread vigorously—consider using containers to avoid its invasive tendencies.

DIRECT SOWING: Sow after danger of frost has passed and when temperatures reach 55°F (13°C).

GERMINATION: 10–14 days

DAYS TO MATURITY: 70–75

POLLINATION: Self, insect

CROSS-POLLINATION: Can cross-pollinate with other varieties. Cage plants or bag blossoms to prevent cross-pollination.

ISOLATION DISTANCE: ¼ mile (0.4 km)

SEED MATURITY: Seeds mature as flower heads brown and dry. Harvest spent flowers and place on a screen to dry further.

SEED PROCESSING: Thresh, rub

SEED VIABILITY: 3 years

TRAITS AND TIPS

LEMON BALM

COMMON NAME: Lemon balm

SCIENTIFIC NAME: *Melissa officinalis*

FAMILY: Lamiaceae

LIFE CYCLE: Perennial

USES: Culinary, medicinal, pollinators, containers, aromatherapy

FRUIT TYPE: Nutlet

SEED-STARTING DEPTH: ⅛" (0.3 cm)

SPECIAL NEEDS: It needs light to germinate. Stratify 1 week prior to germination.

Bee Balm
Monarda spp.

If you garden for wildlife, add bee balm to your list of herbs. Its bright, tall blooms attract bees, naturally, but bee balm also attracts hummingbirds and serves as a host plant for some butterfly larvae. The herb is traditionally used to treat respiratory and digestive conditions, but the purple, pink, or red blooms also add a beautiful statement to floral bouquets.

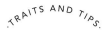

BEE BALM

COMMON NAMES: Bee balm, wild oregano, bergamot

SCIENTIFIC NAMES: *Monarda* spp. (includes *Monarda didyma, M. fistulosa, M. fistulosa* var. *menthifolia, M. punctata, M. citriodora*)

FAMILY: Lamiaceae

LIFE CYCLE: Perennial

USES: Medicinal, pollinators, companion plant, landscape, containers

FRUIT TYPE: Nutlet

SEED-STARTING DEPTH: ⅛" (0.3 cm)

SPECIAL NEEDS: It needs light for germination.

SEED-STARTING SOIL TEMPERATURE: 60–70°F (16–21°C)

SEED START TIMING: Direct sow after frost or start indoors using biodegradable containers 8–10 weeks before last frost.

LIGHT REQUIREMENTS: It needs light to germinate. As seedlings emerge, continue 12–16 hours of light per day.

TRANSPLANT: Plant after danger of frost. Space 12–18" (30–46 cm) apart and ensure good airflow to prevent powdery mildew.

DIRECT SOWING: Sow after danger of frost has passed and when temperatures reach 55°F (13°C).

GERMINATION: 14–30 days

DAYS TO MATURITY: 365 (flowers the second year)

POLLINATION: Insect

CROSS-POLLINATION: Can cross-pollinate with other varieties. Cage plants or bag blossoms to prevent cross-pollination.

ISOLATION DISTANCE: ¼ mile (0.4 km)

SEED MATURITY: Harvest flower clusters when they're dried and brown, about 1–3 weeks after flowering.

SEED PROCESSING: Thresh, flail. (Place seedheads in a paper bag and shake to dislodge seeds.)

SEED VIABILITY: 2 years

Basil
Ocimum basilicum

In my garden, I grow at least a dozen basil varieties, from 'Genovese' and 'Globe' to 'Thai' and 'Dark Purple Opal'. Not only is basil delicious, the plants make perfect companions in the vegetable garden. Beneficial insects adore the blooms, plus basil is thought to repel aphids. Keep basil pinched back during the summer, harvesting it before the stems become woody, and then allow it to flower later in the season to collect seeds.

·TRAITS AND TIPS·

BASIL

COMMON NAMES: Basil, Thai basil, sweet basil, common basil, Holy basil, lemon basil

SCIENTIFIC NAMES: *Ocimum basilicum* (sweet), *O. basilicum* var. *thyrsiflora* (Thai), *O. tenuiflorum* (Holy), *O.* × *citriodorum* (lemon)

FAMILY: Lamiaceae

LIFE CYCLE: Annual

USES: Culinary, medicinal, containers, pollinators, companion planting, landscape

FRUIT TYPE: Nutlet

SEED-STARTING DEPTH: ¼" (0.6 cm)

SPECIAL NEEDS: It needs light for germination.

SEED-STARTING SOIL TEMPERATURE: 68–70°F (20–21°C)

SEED START TIMING: Direct sow after frost. Start indoors using biodegradable containers 6–8 weeks before last frost. Bottom heat speeds germination.

LIGHT REQUIREMENTS: It needs light to germinate. As seedlings emerge, continue 12–16 hours of light per day.

TRANSPLANT: Plant in full sun in well-drained soil after danger of frost. Space 12" (30 cm) apart.

DIRECT SOWING: Sow after danger of frost has passed and when soil temperatures reach 60°F (16°C).

GERMINATION: 7–10 days

DAYS TO MATURITY: 60–90

POLLINATION: Self, insect

CROSS-POLLINATION: Can cross-pollinate with other varieties. Cage plants or bag blossoms to prevent cross-pollination.

ISOLATION DISTANCE: 150' (46 m)

SEED MATURITY: Harvest flower clusters when they are brown.

SEED PROCESSING: Thresh, rub

SEED VIABILITY: 5 years

Oregano and Marjoram
Origanum vulgare,
Origanum majorana

With oregano added to your herb garden, you'll be ready to meet any culinary challenge. While often used interchangeably, oregano and marjoram present different flavors. Oregano's zippy, peppery flavor and pine scent are bolder than marjoram's sweeter, more delicate, and more complex flavor that's filled with floral notes.

OREGANO AND MARJORAM

COMMON NAMES: Oregano, sweet marjoram

SCIENTIFIC NAMES: *Origanum vulgare, Origanum majorana*

FAMILY: Lamiaceae

LIFE CYCLE: Oregano: tender perennial; marjoram: annual

USES: Culinary, medicinal, companion plants, containers, pollinators, borders

FRUIT TYPE: Nutlet

SEED-STARTING DEPTH: ⅛" (0.3 cm)

SPECIAL NEEDS: Stratify 1 week. It needs light for germination.

SEED-STARTING SOIL TEMPERATURE: 68–70°F (20–21°C)

SEED START TIMING: Direct sow after frost. Can be started indoors using biodegradable containers 6–8 weeks before last frost. Bottom heat speeds germination.

LIGHT REQUIREMENTS: It needs light to germinate. As seedlings emerge, continue 12–16 hours of light per day.

TRANSPLANT: Plant in full sun after danger of frost. Space 12" (30 cm) apart.

DIRECT SOWING: Sow after danger of frost has passed and when soil temperatures reach 55°F (13°C).

GERMINATION: 14–21 days

DAYS TO MATURITY: 80–90

POLLINATION: Insect

CROSS-POLLINATION: Can cross-pollinate with other varieties. Cage plants or bag blossoms to prevent cross-pollination.

ISOLATION DISTANCE: ¼ mile (0.4 km)

SEED MATURITY: Seeds are ripe when flower heads turn brown. Harvest the clusters when they're dry.

SEED PROCESSING: Thresh, rub

SEED VIABILITY: 1 year

Parsley
Petroselinum crispum

Interestingly, parsley's place in history included Roman and Greek funeral rites, as well as the Victorian belief that a virgin could not plant parsley or she would become impregnated by the Devil. Parsley's use is a bit more pedestrian these days, often chopped finely and added to dressings or as an ingredient in pesto for a change of pace.

PARSLEY

COMMON NAME: Parsley

SCIENTIFIC NAME: *Petroselinum crispum*

FAMILY: Apiaceae

LIFE CYCLE: Biennial, grown as annual for food

USES: Culinary, medicinal, host plant for pollinator larvae, companion plant, containers

FRUIT TYPE: Schizocarps

SEED-STARTING DEPTH: ¼" (0.6 cm)

SPECIAL NEEDS: Soak seeds overnight prior to planting to speed germination. Plants require vernalization to produce flowers and seeds the second year. Expose plants to temperatures below 50°F (10°C) for 10 weeks, and then replant in spring.

SEED-STARTING SOIL TEMPERATURE: 50–75°F (10–24°C)

SEED START TIMING: Direct sow after frost. Can be started indoors using biodegradable containers 6–8 weeks before last frost.

LIGHT REQUIREMENTS: As soon as seedlings emerge

TRANSPLANT: Plant after danger of frost. Transplanted biennials sometimes bolt, so take care not to disturb roots; using biodegradable pots helps. Space plants 8–10" (20–25 cm) apart.

DIRECT SOWING: Sow after danger of frost has passed and when soil temperatures reach 55°F (13°C).

GERMINATION: 14–30 days

DAYS TO MATURITY: 70–90 for food, second year for seed production

POLLINATION: Insect

CROSS-POLLINATION: Can cross-pollinate with other varieties. Cage plants or bag blossoms to prevent cross-pollination.

ISOLATION DISTANCE: 800'–½ mile (0.24–0.8 km)

SEED MATURITY: Allow umbels to dry on plants. Seeds are ripe and ready for harvest when flower heads turn brown. As seeds mature, place a paper bag over the flower head, tie the bag at its base, and collect seeds as they shatter. Can also remove flower heads and dry on screen.

SEED PROCESSING: Thresh, rub. Winnow to remove debris.

SEED VIABILITY: 2–3 years

ROSEMARY

Rosemary
Rosmarinus officinalis

Rosemary is evergreen in my garden (but not in cold climates, I'm afraid), smells amazing, grows without attention, and blooms profusely in full sun. Medieval brides wore it or included it in their bouquets, as it symbolized happiness, protection, and love.

However, growing rosemary from seed is an exercise in patience. It's not easy. Germination is low, so sow extra seeds. Bottom heat helps with germination, but growth rate is slow. Still, the results are worth the effort, and eventually you'll be enjoying the culinary pleasures of rosemary in your kitchen.

COMMON NAME: Rosemary

SCIENTIFIC NAME: *Rosmarinus officinalis*

FAMILY: Lamiaceae

LIFE CYCLE: Tender perennial

USES: Culinary, medicinal, edible flowers, aromatherapy, pollinators, companion plant, landscape

FRUIT TYPE: Nutlet

SEED-STARTING DEPTH: Surface sow

SPECIAL NEEDS: It needs light to germinate. Bottom heat speeds germination. Note: germination rate is typically low; sow extra seeds.

SEED-STARTING SOIL TEMPERATURE: 80–90°F (27–32°C)

SEED START TIMING: Direct sowing after frost is preferred. Can be started indoors using biodegradable containers 4–5 weeks before last frost. Bottom heat speeds germination. Avoid damping off by providing good air circulation.

LIGHT REQUIREMENTS: It needs light to germinate. As seedlings emerge, continue 12–16 hours of light per day.

TRANSPLANT: Plant after danger of frost. Space 12–15" (30–38 cm) apart where grown as an annual, 24–36" (61–91 cm) where grown as a perennial.

DIRECT SOWING: Sow after danger of frost has passed and when soil temperatures reach 70°F (21°C).

GERMINATION: 14–21 days

DAYS TO MATURITY: 120–180

POLLINATION: Insect

CROSS-POLLINATION: Can cross-pollinate with other varieties. Cage plants or bag blossoms to prevent cross-pollination.

ISOLATION DISTANCE: ½ mile (0.8 km)

SEED MATURITY: Remove flower heads as they turn brown and dry. Spread on screens to dry fully.

SEED PROCESSING: Thresh, rub

SEED VIABILITY: 1 year

Sage and Salvia
Salvia spp.

Comprising nearly 1,000 species, salvia offers many options for gardeners, from culinary, medicinal, and spiritual to ornamental. Pollinators adore salvia, and hummingbirds especially love pineapple sage (*Salvia elegans*), which adds a terrific burst of color in the late-summer garden. Clary sage (*S. sclarea*) is popular for essential oils, while smudging white sage supposedly wards of evil spirits, purifies, and cleanses. Originating from the Latin word *salvere*, meaning "to feel well and healthy," salvia's many uses live up to its name.

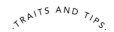

·TRAITS AND TIPS·

SAGE AND SALVIA

COMMON NAMES: Sage, salvia

SCIENTIFIC NAMES: *Salvia officinalis* (common), *S. elegans* (pineapple sage), *S. sclarea* (clary sage), *S. apiana* (white sage), *S. splendens* (scarlet sage)

FAMILY: Lamiaceae

LIFE CYCLE: Perennial, annual, biennial

USES: Culinary, medicinal, containers, landscape, pollinators, attract hummingbirds, companion plant, cut flower, edible flowers

FRUIT TYPE: Nutlet

SEED-STARTING DEPTH: Surface sow

SPECIAL NEEDS: It needs light to germinate. Stratify for 3 weeks.

SEED-STARTING SOIL TEMPERATURE: 75–78°F (24–26°C)

SEED START TIMING: Start indoors using biodegradable containers 8–10 weeks before last frost. Bottom heat speeds germination.

LIGHT REQUIREMENTS: It needs light to germinate. As seedlings emerge, continue 12–16 hours of light per day.

TRANSPLANT: Plant in full sun in well-drained soil after danger of frost. Space 12–24" (30–61 cm) apart depending on variety.

DIRECT SOWING: After danger of frost and when temperatures reach 55°F (13°C).

GERMINATION: 7–21 days

DAYS TO MATURITY: Depends on variety. Annual: 70–85; perennial: 120

POLLINATION: Insect

CROSS-POLLINATION: Can cross-pollinate with other varieties. Cage plants or bag blossoms to prevent cross-pollination.

ISOLATION DISTANCE: ½ mile (0.8 km)

SEED MATURITY: Allow flowers to dry on plants. Harvest flower heads by hand. Seeds are mature when flowers are brown and dry.

SEED PROCESSING: Thresh, flail

SEED VIABILITY: 1 year

Savory, Winter and Summer
Satureja hortensis,
Satureja montana

A popular ingredient in herbes de Provence, a blend of dried herbs used for cooking, savory is also traditionally known as a healing herb, with dual antiseptic and antibacterial properties. However, the difference between winter and summer savory is often confused. Perennial winter savory offers a piney, sharp flavor, while annual summer savory's sweet flavor is more popular with chefs.

TRAITS AND TIPS.
SAVORY

COMMON NAMES: Summer savory, winter savory

SCIENTIFIC NAMES: *Satureja hortensis* (summer), *Satureja montana* (winter)

FAMILY: Lamiaceae

LIFE CYCLE: Summer: annual; winter: perennial

USES: Culinary, medicinal, companion plant, container, border

FRUIT TYPE: Nutlet

SEED-STARTING DEPTH: Surface sow

SPECIAL NEEDS: It needs light to germinate.

SEED-STARTING SOIL TEMPERATURE: 65–70°F (18–21°C)

SEED START TIMING: Start indoors using biodegradable containers 4–6 weeks before last frost. Bottom heat speeds germination.

LIGHT REQUIREMENTS: It needs light to germinate. As seedlings emerge, continue 12–16 hours of light per day.

TRANSPLANT: Plant in full sun in well-drained soil after danger of frost. Space 12" (30 cm) apart for summer savory, 18" (46 cm) apart for winter savory.

DIRECT SOWING: Sow after danger of frost has passed and when soil temperatures reach 65°F (18°C).

GERMINATION: 10–15 days

DAYS TO MATURITY: 60–70

POLLINATION: Insect

CROSS-POLLINATION: Can cross-pollinate with other varieties. Cage plants or bag blossoms to prevent cross-pollination.

ISOLATION DISTANCE: ½ mile (0.8 km)

SEED MATURITY: Allow flower heads to dry on plants. Harvest and spread on screens to dry fully.

SEED PROCESSING: Thresh

SEED VIABILITY: 3 years

Stevia
Stevia rebaudiana

Growing the stevia plant provides an easy way to ensure that you're using a natural ingredient to sweeten your drinks and treats without adding chemicals or calories. Germination rate is low, so sow additional seeds. Use stevia fresh, dry, or powdered to replace sugar in teas, sorbets, and even baked goods.

STEVIA

COMMON NAME: Stevia

SCIENTIFIC NAME: *Stevia rebaudiana*

FAMILY: Asteraceae

LIFE CYCLE: Tender perennial (does not tolerate temperatures below 45°F (7°C)

USES: Culinary, medicinal, containers, companion plant

FRUIT TYPE: Achene

SEED-STARTING DEPTH: ⅛" (0.3 cm)

SPECIAL NEEDS: Typically has low germination rates; sow extra seeds.

SEED-STARTING SOIL TEMPERATURE: 68–75°F (20–24°C)

SEED START TIMING: Start indoors using biodegradable containers 8–10 weeks before last frost. Bottom heat speeds germination.

LIGHT REQUIREMENTS: As soon as seedlings emerge

TRANSPLANT: Plant in full sun in well-drained soil after danger of frost. Plants prefer moist but not wet locations. Space 12" (30 cm) apart. Pinch plants to encourage branching.

DIRECT SOWING: Sow after danger of frost has passed and when soil temperatures reach 65°F (18°C).

GERMINATION: 7–21 days

DAYS TO MATURITY: 100–120

POLLINATION: Insect

CROSS-POLLINATION: Can cross-pollinate with other varieties, but incidence is low. Cage plants or bag blossoms to prevent cross-pollination as a precaution.

ISOLATION DISTANCE: ¼ mile (0.4 km)

SEED MATURITY: Dry flower heads on plants or harvest prior to frost and allow flowers to continue to dry fully. Harvest seeds when the flower head is completely dry.

SEED PROCESSING: Thresh

SEED VIABILITY: 1 year

Thyme
Thymus vulgaris

Thyme matures slowly so start it from seed early. Not only does it add delicious flavor to your culinary creations, thyme's edible flowers add a creative treat to dishes. Traditionally, thyme has been used to support the immune system and is thought to aid digestion and respiratory issues. Pollinators love the blooms so leave a few flowers for them to enjoy, and you'll have seeds to harvest as well.

THYME

COMMON NAME: Thyme

SCIENTIFIC NAME: *Thymus vulgaris*

FAMILY: Lamiaceae

LIFE CYCLE: Perennial

USES: Culinary, medicinal, companion plant, container, border, pollinators, edible flowers

FRUIT TYPE: Nutlet

SEED-STARTING DEPTH: Surface sow

SPECIAL NEEDS: It needs light to germinate. Bottom heat speeds germination. Provide good air circulation to avoid damping off.

SEED-STARTING SOIL TEMPERATURE: 60–70°F (16–21°C)

SEED START TIMING: Start indoors using biodegradable containers 14–16 weeks before last frost. Bottom heat speeds germination.

LIGHT REQUIREMENTS: It needs light to germinate. As seedlings emerge, continue 12–16 hours of light per day.

TRANSPLANT: Plant in full sun in well-drained soil after danger of frost. Space 9–15" (23–38 cm) apart. Benefits from part shade in hot climates.

DIRECT SOWING: Sow after danger of frost has passed and when soil temperatures reach 60°F (16°C). Indoor starting is recommended.

GERMINATION: 14–21 days

DAYS TO MATURITY: 90–95

POLLINATION: Insect

CROSS-POLLINATION: Can cross-pollinate with other varieties. Cage plants or bag blossoms to prevent cross-pollination.

ISOLATION DISTANCE: ½ mile (0.8 km)

SEED MATURITY: Dry flowers on plants or harvest prior to frost and allow flower heads to continue to dry fully. Harvest seeds when the flower is brown and dry.

SEED PROCESSING: Thresh, rub

SEED VIABILITY: 3 years

Flowers

My earliest memories include my mother gently squeezing a plastic plant cell as she turned it over, loosening a petunia from the tray and placing it in my hand. I held it reverently, afraid the flower would die in the short intermission from cellpack to my hand to soil, waiting anxiously for my mom to dig the hole where I'd place the plant.

Today I grow many flowers from seeds, tucking them into the kitchen garden as companion plants, filling containers to overflow with blooms, and allocating beds to cutting gardens. Growing my own flowers ensures that they're raised the way I want them to be: organic and without chemicals and pesticides that can harm pollinators. While growing vegetables and herbs provides many practical benefits, like feeding yourself and your family, growing flowers marries practicality with aesthetic pleasure. Really, is there anything nicer than receiving or giving a mood-brightening, heartfelt bouquet of homegrown blooms?

Snapdragon
Antirrhinum majus

Do you remember pinching snapdragon heads as a child, making them open their "mouths"? Snapdragons remind me of childhood, those lazy days of roaming outside. In my warm climate, I plant them in the fall as they tolerate light frost and bloom best in cooler temperatures. Add these to your cutting garden as they make a lovely addition to bouquets. Its flowers are edible—but not tasty!

SNAPDRAGON

COMMON NAME: Snapdragon

SCIENTIFIC NAME: *Antirrhinum majus*

FAMILY: Scrophulariaceae

LIFE CYCLE: Annual

USES: Cut flower, landscape, containers, pollinators, companion plant, cottage garden

FRUIT TYPE: Capsule

SEED-STARTING DEPTH: Surface sow

SPECIAL NEEDS: Stratify for 1–2 weeks.

SEED-STARTING SOIL TEMPERATURE: 65–70°F (18–21°C)

SEED START TIMING: Start indoors using biodegradable containers 10–12 weeks before last frost. Keep soil moist. Can also sow indoors in warm climates during late summer for a fall planting.

LIGHT REQUIREMENTS: As soon as seedlings emerge

TRANSPLANT: Plant in full sun in well-drained soil after danger of frost. Pinch tops off when seedlings reach 3–4" (8–10 cm) to encourage branching. Space 6–12" (15–30 cm) apart. Snapdragons bloom best in cooler temperatures.

DIRECT SOWING: Sow after danger of frost has passed and when temperatures reach 55°F (13°C).

GERMINATION: 8–14 days

DAYS TO MATURITY: 80–100

POLLINATION: Self, insect

CROSS-POLLINATION: Can cross-pollinate with other varieties. Cage plants or bag blossoms to prevent cross-pollination.

ISOLATION DISTANCE: 600' (183 m)

SEED MATURITY: Seed capsules ripen from the base of an inflorescence upward. Handpick dry pods or cut flower spikes when the majority of pods are dry. (A second flower spike may form to extend bloom life.) Dry on screens.

SEED PROCESSING: Thresh, flail

SEED VIABILITY: 3–4 years

Columbine
Aquilegia spp.

One of my favorite spring blooms, columbines not only attract pollinators but they are also a favorite food source of hummingbirds. Their delicate blooms and nodding heads add an adorable charm to woodland gardens and borders.

COLUMBINE

COMMON NAME: Columbine

SCIENTIFIC NAME: *Aquilegia* spp.

FAMILY: Ranunculaceae

LIFE CYCLE: Perennial

USES: Cut flower, landscape, pollinator, woodland, border, containers, attract hummingbirds

FRUIT TYPE: Follicle

SEED-STARTING DEPTH: ⅛" (0.3 cm)

SPECIAL NEEDS: Sow in trays or pots and stratify at 40°F (4°C) for 3 weeks. (A refrigerator works well.) Keep soil moist and place under lights after stratification. It needs light to germinate.

SEED-STARTING SOIL TEMPERATURE: 65–75°F (18–24°C)

SEED START TIMING: Start indoors using trays or biodegradable containers 8–10 weeks before last frost.

LIGHT REQUIREMENTS: It needs light to germinate. As seedlings emerge, continue 12–16 hours of light per day.

TRANSPLANT: Plant in light shade in well-drained, humus-rich soil after danger of frost. Space 12" (30 cm) apart. Taller varieties may need staking.

DIRECT SOWING: Sow after danger of frost has passed and when temperatures reach 55°F (13°C). Can also direct sow in fall for natural stratification.

GERMINATION: 21–28 days

DAYS TO MATURITY: Plants bloom the second year

POLLINATION: Insect

CROSS-POLLINATION: Can cross-pollinate with other varieties. Cage plants or bag blossoms to prevent cross-pollination.

ISOLATION DISTANCE: ¼ mile (0.4 km)

SEED MATURITY: Seeds are mature when flower heads fully dry and form follicles. Dry on plants or harvest and dry on screens. Seeds should be dark green or almost black at harvest.

SEED PROCESSING: Thresh

SEED VIABILITY: 2 years

Milkweed
Asclepias spp.

Milkweed, the bane of farmers and a previously pesky roadside weed, rose to fame as efforts to save the monarch butterfly drew attention to this important host plant for monarch larvae. While some controversy still exists about whether certain varieties should be planted in warmer regions, the efforts of gardeners and conservation groups to save the monarch have made milkweed a popular addition to gardens.

MILKWEED

COMMON NAMES: Milkweed, butterfly weed, pleurisy root

SCIENTIFIC NAME: *Asclepias* spp.

FAMILY: Asclepiadaceae

LIFE CYCLE: Perennial

USES: Medicinal, pollinators, landscape, containers, companion plant; famous as host plant for monarch butterfly larvae

FRUIT TYPE: Follicle

SEED-STARTING DEPTH: ¼" (0.6 cm)

SPECIAL NEEDS: Stratify 6–10 weeks to improve germination.

SEED-STARTING SOIL TEMPERATURE: 65–70°F (18–21°C)

SEED START TIMING: Direct sow in fall for natural stratification. Can be started indoors using biodegradable containers 10–12 weeks before last frost.

LIGHT REQUIREMENTS: As soon as seedlings emerge

TRANSPLANT: Plant after danger of frost. Do not disturb roots. Space 12–24" (30–61 cm) apart, depending on variety and size.

DIRECT SOWING: Sow in fall for natural stratification.

GERMINATION: 14–21 days if seeds are stratified. Germination is slow.

DAYS TO MATURITY: Blooms its second year.

POLLINATION: Insect

CROSS-POLLINATION: Can cross-pollinate with other varieties. Cage plants or bag blossoms to prevent cross-pollination.

ISOLATION DISTANCE: ½ mile (0.8 km)

SEED MATURITY: Dry pods on plants. Seeds are mature when a pod is completely dry and begins to split. Seeds are brown at maturity. If seeds are green, they are not ready to harvest. Avoid pods with milkweed bugs as the insects can pierce the pod and feed on the seeds. Collect follicles as they ripen and begin to split. Place on a screen to dry fully.

SEED PROCESSING: Try to harvest follicles by hand before they're fully open for ease of extracting seeds from fibers; otherwise, you'll have a blowsy puff of fibers, making seed extraction challenging. Grasp a bundle of floss fibers at the tapered end of follicle. Separate seeds from floss by rubbing. Discard the floss and shells.

SEED VIABILITY: 2–3 years

Aster

Aster amellus, Almutaster, Canadanthus, Doellingeria, Eucephalus, Eurybia, Ionactis, Oligoneuron, Oreostemma, Sericocarpus, and *Symphyotricum; Callistephus chinensis*

Asters serve as the stars of the fall garden, providing fresh blooms and color when summer flowers fade. Ranging in height from dwarf to more than 6 feet, you'll find many varieties to meet your garden needs, whether it's as a border or as part of a cutting garden.

DNA studies showed that North American asters are quite different from those in Eurasia, which led to an aster reclassification in the 1990s. It's very confusing, honestly. The good news is that most asters, along with what a friend calls "ex-asters" and China asters, grow very similarly from seed, although they may serve different purposes. China asters are annuals used extensively in the floral industry as cut flowers. *Aster amellus,* along with the newer genera reclassifications of *Almutaster, Canadanthus, Doellingeria, Eucephalus, Eurybia, Ionactis, Oligoneuron, Oreostemma, Sericocarpus,* and *Symphyotricum* provide a beautiful fall woodland or meadow feel, aiding pollinators in their search for food as other flowers fade. Check your seed varieties to determine what you're growing, but as long as the plant is open pollinated, you can save seeds from all these beauties.

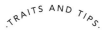

TRAITS AND TIPS

ASTER

COMMON NAMES: Aster, frost flower, starwort, Michaelmas Daisy

SCIENTIFIC NAMES: *Aster amellus, Almutaster, Canadanthus, Doellingeria, Eucephalus, Eurybia, Ionactis, Oligoneuron, Oreostemma, Sericocarpus,* and *Symphyotricum* (asters and reclassifications), *Callistephus chinensis* (China aster)

FAMILY: Asteraceae

LIFE CYCLE: Perennial; *Callistephus chinensis,* annual

USES: Pollinators, landscape, woodland, meadow, medicinal, cut flower, borders (dwarf)

FRUIT TYPE: Achene-like cypsela

SEED-STARTING DEPTH: ¼" (0.6 cm)

SPECIAL NEEDS: It's prone to damping off; provide good air circulation.

SEED-STARTING SOIL TEMPERATURE: 60–70°F (16–21°C)

SEED START TIMING: Direct sow after frost. Can be started indoors using biodegradable containers 6–8 weeks before last frost.

LIGHT REQUIREMENTS: As soon as seedlings emerge

TRANSPLANT: Plant in full sun in well-drained soil after danger of frost. Space 4–6" (10–15 cm) apart for smaller varieties, 12–24" (30–61 cm) apart for tall varieties.

DIRECT SOWING: Sow after danger of frost has passed and when soil temperatures reach 55°F (13°C).

GERMINATION: 10–14 days

DAYS TO MATURITY: Perennials bloom second year; annual China aster blooms 110–120 days after sowing.

POLLINATION: Insect

CROSS-POLLINATION: Can cross-pollinate with other varieties. Cage plants or bag blossoms to prevent cross-pollination.

ISOLATION DISTANCE: ½ mile (0.8 km)

SEED MATURITY: Seeds are mature when flower heads are dry and brown. Handpick and spread on screens to dry.

SEED PROCESSING: Flail, rub

SEED VIABILITY: 1–2 years

Bellflower
Campanula

For such an adorable flower, bellflower received some bad press historically because the plant was associated with witches. (It even sported the name "Witches' Thimble.") However, there's nothing sinister about bellflower. Its clusters of bell-shaped blooms feed pollinators and add brightness to the garden.

·TRAITS AND TIPS·

BELLFLOWER

COMMON NAME: Bellflower

SCIENTIFIC NAME: *Campanula* spp.

FAMILY: Campanulaceae

LIFE CYCLE: Perennial, biennial, annual

USES: Landscape, pollinators, containers, cut flower, woodland garden

FRUIT TYPE: Capsule

SEED-STARTING DEPTH: Surface sow

SPECIAL NEEDS: Stratify 3 weeks prior to sowing. It needs light to germinate.

SEED-STARTING SOIL TEMPERATURE: 70–75°F (21–24°C)

SEED START TIMING: Direct sow after frost or start indoors 10–12 weeks before last frost. Bottom heat speeds germination.

LIGHT REQUIREMENTS: It needs light to germinate. As seedlings emerge, continue 12–16 hours of light per day.

TRANSPLANT: Plant in full or part sun in well-drained soil after danger of frost. Space 12" (30 cm) apart.

DIRECT SOWING: Sow after danger of frost has passed and when soil temperatures reach 60°F (16°C).

GERMINATION: 14–21 days

DAYS TO MATURITY: Perennial: blooms second year; annual: 120–140

POLLINATION: Insect

CROSS-POLLINATION: Can cross-pollinate with other varieties. Cage plants or bag blossoms to prevent cross-pollination.

ISOLATION DISTANCE: ¼ mile (0.4km)

SEED MATURITY: Spread flower spikes on screens to dry fully.

SEED PROCESSING: Flail, thresh

SEED VIABILITY: 3 years

Love-in-a-Puff
Cardiospermum halicabum

The first time I saw love-in-a-puff on a trellis in a restaurant's kitchen garden, it was covered by bees. They flitted from each tiny flower to the next, like someone threw a bee soirée. Not only is it a great pollinator plant, but the vine adds interest to the garden with "puffs" that resemble miniature paper lanterns. The best part is within each "puff" resides a dark seed, decorated with a perfect cream-colored heart. Thus, love-in-a-puff—a perfect name for a spectacular plant.

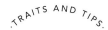

LOVE-IN-A-PUFF

COMMON NAMES: Love-in-a-puff, balloon vine, winter cherry

SCIENTIFIC NAME: *Cardiospermum halicabum*

FAMILY: Sapindaceae

LIFE CYCLE: Tender perennial vine

USES: Pollinators, landscape, vertical interest, trellises, cut flower, companion plant, culinary, medicinal. Note: can be invasive in warm areas; check before planting.

FRUIT TYPE: Capsule

SEED-STARTING DEPTH: ½" (1.3 cm)

SPECIAL NEEDS: 65–70°F (18–21°C)

SEED START TIMING: Start indoors using biodegradable containers 8–10 weeks before last frost.

LIGHT REQUIREMENTS: As soon as seedlings emerge

TRANSPLANT: Plant in full sun in well-drained soil after danger of frost. Space 6–12" (15–30 cm). Plants grow 6–10' (1.8–3 m) and need trellising.

DIRECT SOWING: Sow after danger of frost has passed and when temperatures reach 55°F (13°C).

GERMINATION: 21–30 days

DAYS TO MATURITY: 120

POLLINATION: Insect

CROSS-POLLINATION: Can cross-pollinate with other varieties. Cage plants or bag blossoms to prevent cross-pollination.

ISOLATION DISTANCE: ½ mile (0.8 km)

SEED MATURITY: Allow fruit to dry completely on the vines.

SEED PROCESSING: Hand, thresh

SEED VIABILITY: 1 year

Celosia/Cockscomb
Celosia spp.

Celosia, which is also called cockscomb, create a conversation piece, whether it's the coral-shaped cristata type, the candlelike spicata type, or the flame-shaped plumosa type. (Personally, I always call the cristata type the "brain" flower due to its appearance.)

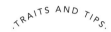

COMMON NAMES: Celosia, cockscomb

SCIENTIFIC NAME: *Celosia* spp.

FAMILY: Amaranthaceae

LIFE CYCLE: Annual; *C. roripifolia*, biennial

USES: Landscape, pollinators, cut flower, borders

FRUIT TYPE: Capsule

SEED-STARTING DEPTH: Surface sow

SPECIAL NEEDS: It needs light for germination.

SEED-STARTING SOIL TEMPERATURE: 70–80°F (21–27°C)

SEED START TIMING: Direct sow after frost. Can be started indoors 8–10 weeks before last frost. Bottom heat speeds germination.

LIGHT REQUIREMENTS: It needs light to germinate. As seedlings emerge, continue 12–16 hours of light per day.

TRANSPLANT: Plant in rich, well-drained soil after danger of frost. Space 6–12" (15–30 cm) apart depending on variety. Pinch seedlings to encourage branching.

DIRECT SOWING: Sow after danger of frost has passed and when soil temperatures reach 65°F (18°C).

GERMINATION: 7–14 days

DAYS TO MATURITY: 90–120

POLLINATION: Insect, wind

CROSS-POLLINATION: Can cross-pollinate with other varieties. Cage plants or bag blossoms to prevent cross-pollination.

ISOLATION DISTANCE: ¼ mile (0.4 km)

SEED MATURITY: Harvest the spent, dry flower heads. Place on screens to dry fully.

SEED PROCESSING: Flail

SEED VIABILITY: 4–5 years

Bachelor's Buttons/ Cornflower
Centaurea cyanus

In Victorian times, unencumbered bachelors wore this bright blue flower in their buttonhole to indicate that they were single and available, leading to the name "Bachelor's Buttons." Today, the cheerful blue, pink, red, or white flowers make a perfect addition to a wildflower or cutting garden.

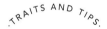

COMMON NAMES: Bachelor's Buttons, cornflower

SCIENTIFIC NAME: *Centaurea cyanus*

FAMILY: Asteraceae

LIFE CYCLE: Perennial and annual

USES: Borders, landscape, cut flower, pollinators, companion plant, meadow

FRUIT TYPE: Achenes

SEED-STARTING DEPTH: ¼" (0.6 cm)

SPECIAL NEEDS: Stratify for 1 week. Germinate in darkness.

SEED-STARTING SOIL TEMPERATURE: 70–75°F (21–24°C)

SEED START TIMING: Direct sow after frost or start indoors 8–10 weeks before last frost. Bottom heat speeds germination.

LIGHT REQUIREMENTS: As soon as seedlings emerge

TRANSPLANT: Plant in full sun in well-drained soil after danger of frost. Space 12–24" (30–61 cm) apart.

DIRECT SOWING: Sow after danger of frost has passed and when soil temperatures reach 55°F (13°C).

GERMINATION: 7–28 days

DAYS TO MATURITY: 80–95

POLLINATION: Insect

CROSS-POLLINATION: Can cross-pollinate with other varieties. Cage plants or bag blossoms to prevent cross-pollination.

ISOLATION DISTANCE: ¼ mile (0.4 km)

SEED MATURITY: Harvest flowers as they fade and dry. Birds love the seeds, so harvest promptly or protect with bird netting. Fruits shatter easily.

SEED PROCESSING: Thresh, flail

SEED VIABILITY: 3–5 years

Cleome
Cleome hassleriana

Looking for a deer-resistant plant? Cleome may suit your needs. The fragrance of cleome doesn't appeal to everyone, though, and it can be a bit sticky when you're handling it, so consider wearing gloves. Its prolific blooms add a nice burst of color to the summer garden when other flowers look tired.

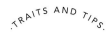

CLEOME

COMMON NAMES: Cleome, spider flower

SCIENTIFIC NAME: *Cleome hassleriana*

FAMILY: Capparaceae

LIFE CYCLE: Annual

USES: Landscape, pollinators, cut flower, containers, companion plant

FRUIT TYPE: Capsule

SEED-STARTING DEPTH: ¼" (0.6 cm)

SPECIAL NEEDS: Stratify 2 weeks. Germination is best when grown at 80°F (27°C) during the day and 70°F (21°C) at night. Use a heat mat and lower the temperature at night (or turn it off).

SEED-STARTING SOIL TEMPERATURE: 70–80°F (21–27°C)

SEED START TIMING: Direct sow after frost. Can be started indoors 6–8 weeks before last frost. Bottom heat speeds germination.

LIGHT REQUIREMENTS: As soon as seedlings emerge

TRANSPLANT: Plant in full sun in well-drained soil after danger of frost. Space 12" (30 cm) apart. May need staking or support.

DIRECT SOWING: Sow after danger of frost has passed and when soil temperatures reach 60°F (16°C).

GERMINATION: 7–14 days

DAYS TO MATURITY: 70–80

POLLINATION: Insect

CROSS-POLLINATION: Can cross-pollinate with other varieties. Cage plants or bag blossoms to prevent cross-pollination.

ISOLATION DISTANCE: ¼ mile (0.4 km)

SEED MATURITY: Harvest seedheads when capsules turn brown; place on screen to dry.

SEED PROCESSING: Flail

SEED VIABILITY: 1 year

Coreopsis
Coreopsis spp.

Coreopsis is known in the language of flowers as "always cheerful," and it's true. Its bright, daisylike blooms not only add a burst of sunniness to the garden, but they attract goldfinches, which adore their seeds. (Make sure to bag some of the seedheads so that the birds don't eat your seed supply for next year.) With more than one hundred varieties, you'll find a perfect species to fill your borders, containers, or vases.

COREOPSIS

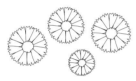

COMMON NAMES: Coreopsis, tickseed, pot of gold

SCIENTIFIC NAME: *Coreopsis* spp.

FAMILY: Asteraceae

LIFE CYCLE: Annual, perennial

USES: Prairie gardens, landscape, pollinators, companion plant

FRUIT TYPE: Achenes

SEED-STARTING DEPTH: ⅛" (0.3 cm)

SPECIAL NEEDS: Stratify 3–4 weeks. It needs light to germinate.

SEED-STARTING SOIL TEMPERATURE: 55–70°F (13–21°C)

SEED START TIMING: Direct sow after frost. Can be started indoors 8–10 weeks before last frost.

LIGHT REQUIREMENTS: It needs light to germinate. As seedlings emerge, continue 12–16 hours of light per day.

TRANSPLANT: Plant after danger of frost. Do not disturb roots. Space 15–18" (38–46 cm) for smaller varieties, 24–30" (61–76 cm) for larger varieties.

DIRECT SOWING: Sow after danger of frost has passed and when temperatures reach 55°F (13°C).

GERMINATION: 14–28 days

DAYS TO MATURITY: Annual: 70–80; perennial: blooms the second year

POLLINATION: Insect

CROSS-POLLINATION: Can cross-pollinate with other varieties. Cage plants or bag blossoms to prevent cross-pollination.

ISOLATION DISTANCE: ½ mile (0.8 km)

SEED MATURITY: Harvest when flowers are faded and dry. Seeds ripen unevenly; spread flowers on screens to dry fully. Goldfinches enjoy the seed, so harvest promptly or use bird netting.

SEED PROCESSING: Thresh, hand

SEED VIABILITY: 2–3 years

Cosmos
Cosmos bipinnatus,
C. sulphureus

Ah, cosmos . . . what would a garden be without the many varieties of this lovely summer and fall annual? A perfect cut flower, companion plant, pollinator magnet, and landscape addition, cosmos is a workhorse in the garden. If you're anxious about seed starting and saving, this is where you should begin, as cosmos will not disappoint. Try one of my favorite varieties, *C. bipinnatus* 'Sea Shell'. Its unique tubular petals add interest to the garden.

COSMOS

COMMON NAMES: Cosmos, Mexican aster, cut-leaf cosmos

SCIENTIFIC NAMES: *Cosmos bipinnatus, C. sulphureus*

FAMILY: Asteraceae

LIFE CYCLE: Annual

USES: Cut flower, pollinators, landscape, companion plant, cottage garden

FRUIT TYPE: Achene

SEED-STARTING DEPTH: ¼" (0.6 cm)

SPECIAL NEEDS: None

SEED-STARTING SOIL TEMPERATURE: 65–75°F (18–24°C)

SEED START TIMING: Direct sow after frost preferred. Can be started indoors using biodegradable containers 4–6 weeks before last frost. Bottom heat speeds germination.

LIGHT REQUIREMENTS: As soon as seedlings emerge

TRANSPLANT: Plant in full sun in well-drained soil after danger of frost. Once established, plants can tolerate poor soil and drought conditions. Space 9–12" (23–30 cm) apart. May need staking.

DIRECT SOWING: Sow after danger of frost has passed and when soil temperatures reach 60°F (16°C).

GERMINATION: 7–10 days

DAYS TO MATURITY: 90–110

POLLINATION: Insect

CROSS-POLLINATION: Can cross-pollinate with other varieties. Cage plants or bag blossoms to prevent cross-pollination.

ISOLATION DISTANCE: ¼ mile (0.4 km)

SEED MATURITY: Dry flower heads on plants or harvest seedheads as flowers dry and place on screens until fully dry.

SEED PROCESSING: Rub, thresh

SEED VIABILITY: 5 years

Dianthus
Dianthus spp.

With more than three hundred species, there's a perfect dianthus for your needs, whether you want to create bouquets with carnations, border a walkway with pinks, or add sweet William to your cutting garden. Carnations are experiencing a resurgence of interest in the floral industry due to the new, beautiful varieties available. All dianthus plants offer many benefits to pollinators in your garden.

DIANTHUS

COMMON NAMES: Dianthus, sweet William, carnation, pinks

SCIENTIFIC NAMES: *Dianthus* spp. (*D. barbatus*, sweet William; *D. plumarius*, Pinks; *D. caryophyllus*, carnation)

FAMILY: Caryophyllaceae

LIFE CYCLE: Annual, perennial

USES: Cut flower, borders, landscape, pollinators, companion plant, edible flowers

FRUIT TYPE: Capsule (valvate)

SEED-STARTING DEPTH: Surface sow

SPECIAL NEEDS: Some varieties, like *D. caryophllus*, need stratification at 39°F (4°C) for 2 weeks to germinate.

SEED-STARTING SOIL TEMPERATURE: 60–70°F (16–21°C)

SEED START TIMING: Start indoors 8–10 weeks before last frost.

LIGHT REQUIREMENTS: As soon as seedlings emerge

TRANSPLANT: Plant in full sun after danger of frost. Space 6–12" (15–30 cm) apart, depending on the variety.

DIRECT SOWING: Sow after danger of frost has passed and when soil temperatures reach 55°F (13°C).

GERMINATION: 14–21 days

DAYS TO MATURITY: 110–140, depending on variety

POLLINATION: Insect

CROSS-POLLINATION: Can cross-pollinate with other varieties. Cage plants or bag blossoms to prevent cross-pollination.

ISOLATION DISTANCE: ¼ mile (0.4 km)

SEED MATURITY: Harvest whole plants and handpick dried capsules. Spread capsules on screens to dry. Capsules can shatter easily.

SEED PROCESSING: Rub, flail

SEED VIABILITY: 3 years

Blanket Flower
Gaillardia spp.

Did the name "blanket flower" originate because of the ability of *Gaillardia* to cover garden beds with its spreading habit and bright blooms, or was it the resemblance of its yellow-and-red flowers to the brightly patterned blankets of Native Americans? Experts are divided about the name's origin, but gardeners agree that *Gaillardia* is a perfect plant to add to your garden to attract pollinators.

BLANKET FLOWER

COMMON NAME: Blanket flower

SCIENTIFIC NAME: *Gaillardia* spp.

FAMILY: Asteraceae

LIFE CYCLE: Annual, perennial

USES: Landscape, pollinators, cut flower, companion plant, medicinal

FRUIT TYPE: Achenes

SEED-STARTING DEPTH: Surface sow

SPECIAL NEEDS: It needs light to germinate.

SEED-STARTING SOIL TEMPERATURE: 70–75°F (21–24°C) during day, 60–65°F (16–18°C) at night

SEED START TIMING: Direct sow in fall. Can be started indoors 6–8 weeks before last frost.

LIGHT REQUIREMENTS: It needs light to germinate. As seedlings emerge, continue 12–16 hours of light per day.

TRANSPLANT: Plant in full sun after danger of frost. Space 6–12" (15–30 cm) apart, depending on variety.

DIRECT SOWING: Sow after danger of frost has passed and when soil temperatures reach 55°F (13°C).

GERMINATION: 14–21 days

DAYS TO MATURITY: 90–120

POLLINATION: Insect

CROSS-POLLINATION: Can cross-pollinate with other varieties. Cage plants or bag blossoms to prevent cross-pollination.

ISOLATION DISTANCE: ¼ mile (0.4 km)

SEED MATURITY: Harvest when flowers turn brown and petals fall off. Dry seedheads on screens.

SEED PROCESSING: Flail, hand (wear gloves)

SEED VIABILITY: 2–4 years

Geranium
Geranium spp., *Pelargonium*x spp.

The geranium conundrum: It's another one of those pesky, confusing plants with multiple names. (It's also one of the reasons to know scientific names when ordering seeds.) Once upon a time, the upright, garden center annual geraniums and the perennial cranesbill belonged in the same classification. However, that's no longer true. When we talk about colorful geraniums, those are annuals that belong to the scientific classification of *Pelargonium*. Hardy geraniums, like cranesbill, that are popular in rock gardens or woodland plantings, belong to the true Geraniaceae classification. However, because of the overlap in names, I've included them both here, as many people don't distinguish the difference in scientific names. The main differences to note are when to start the seeds and germination time.

GERANIUM

COMMON NAMES: Geranium, cranesbill

SCIENTIFIC NAMES: *Geranium* spp., *Pelargonium* spp.

FAMILY: Geraniaceae

LIFE CYCLE: Annual, perennial

USES: Containers, landscape, pollinators, rock gardens, borders

FRUIT TYPE: Schizocarp *(Geranium)*, capsule *(Pelargonium)*

SEED-STARTING DEPTH: ⅛" (0.3 cm)

SPECIAL NEEDS: Geraniums are slow to germinate. Don't prematurely discard them. Seeds need stratification. Keep moist, as it may take months for seeds to germinate.

SEED-STARTING SOIL TEMPERATURE: 70–75°F (21–24°C)

SEED START TIMING: Start indoors 12–16 weeks before last frost for *Geranium*, 8–10 weeks for *Pelargonium*.

LIGHT REQUIREMENTS: As soon as seedlings emerge

TRANSPLANT: Plant in full sun in well-drained soil after danger of frost. Space 12" (30 cm) apart.

DIRECT SOWING: Sow after danger of frost has passed and when soil temperatures reach 55°F (13°C).

GERMINATION: *Geranium*, 30–60 days; *Pelargonium*, 7–14 days

DAYS TO MATURITY: 84–120

POLLINATION: Insect

CROSS-POLLINATION: Can cross-pollinate with other varieties. Cage plants or bag blossoms to prevent cross-pollination.

ISOLATION DISTANCE: ¼ mile (0.4 km)

SEED MATURITY: Collect fruit when flowers turn dry and brown. Handpick and place on screens to dry completely.

SEED PROCESSING: Rub, flail

SEED VIABILITY: 2–3 years

Sunflower
Helianthus spp.

One of the best flowers for beginning the seed-starting and -saving journey, sunflowers offer a great sense of accomplishment. From the towering stalks that fill your landscape with cheer to the perennial plants that add more delicate, ethereal blooms, sunflowers are easy to grow, delightful in bouquets, and simple for seed saving. (Just make certain you beat the birds and squirrels to the seedheads or bag a few blooms to save the seeds from becoming wildlife snacks.) Note: Plant breeders created pollen-less hybrid varieties used most often by florists. If you wish to avoid pollen on your dining room placemats, you may want to invest in growing a few hybrid varieties for floral arrangements. (Remember, though, you won't want to save these seeds, as the next generation of plants most likely won't be true to the parent.)

SUNFLOWER

COMMON NAME: Sunflower

SCIENTIFIC NAME: *Helianthus* spp.

FAMILY: Asteraceae

LIFE CYCLE: Perennial and Annual

USES: Cut flower, pollinators, culinary, landscape, cottage garden, meadow, companion plant

FRUIT TYPE: Achene

SEED-STARTING DEPTH: ½" (1.3 cm)

SPECIAL NEEDS: Perennial varieties need stratification for 12 weeks at 41°F (5°C).

SEED-STARTING SOIL TEMPERATURE: 70–75°F (21–24°C)

SEED START TIMING: Direct sowing after frost is preferred. Can be started indoors using biodegradable containers 4–5 weeks before last frost.

LIGHT REQUIREMENTS: As soon as seedlings emerge.

TRANSPLANT: Plant in full sun after danger of frost. Do not disturb roots. Space 4–24" (10–61 cm) apart, depending on variety.

DIRECT SOWING: Sow after danger of frost has passed and when soil temperatures reach 55°F (13°C).

GERMINATION: 14–21 days

DAYS TO MATURITY: 90–120

POLLINATION: Insect

CROSS-POLLINATION: Can cross-pollinate with other varieties. Cage plants or bag blossoms to prevent cross-pollination.

ISOLATION DISTANCE: ½ mile (0.8 km)

SEED MATURITY: Harvest seeds when flowers dry and seeds are dark colored and rub off easily. Harvest drying flowers and hang them upside down to dry completely.

SEED PROCESSING: Thresh, rub. Dry seeds for 2 more weeks prior to storage.

SEED VIABILITY: 2–3 years

Moonflower and Morning Glory
Ipomoea spp.

The lovely plants of moonflower and morning glory share many characteristics: They develop vines that can grow to 12 feet or more, their flowers bloom only shortly, and pollinators love their flowers. However, the many varieties of morning glory flowers open in the morning and close in the evening, while moonflower's white blooms open at night and close by morning. Be aware that *Ipomoea* spp. can be invasive in some climates. Check before planting.

MOONFLOWER AND MORNING GLORY

COMMON NAMES: Moonflower, morning glory, cyprus vine

SCIENTIFIC NAMES: *Ipomoea alba* (moonflower), *I. purpurea* (morning glory), *I. quamoclit* (cypress vine)

FAMILY: Convolvulaceae

LIFE CYCLE: Annual

USES: Landscape, pollinators, containers, moon garden (moonflowers)

FRUIT TYPE: Capsule

SEED-STARTING DEPTH: ½" (1.3 cm)

SPECIAL NEEDS: Scarify, then soak seeds for 24 hours in water prior to planting.

SEED-STARTING SOIL TEMPERATURE: 70–75°F (21–24°C)

SEED START TIMING: Direct sowing after frost is preferred. Can be started indoors using biodegradable containers 3–4 weeks before last frost.

LIGHT REQUIREMENTS: As soon as seedlings emerge

TRANSPLANT: Plant after danger of frost. Do not disturb roots. Space 10–12" apart and trellis, as vines can reach 8–12' (2–4 m).

DIRECT SOWING: Sow after danger of frost has passed and when soil temperatures reach 60°F (16°C).

GERMINATION: 21–28 days

DAYS TO MATURITY: 75–110

POLLINATION: Insect

CROSS-POLLINATION: Can cross-pollinate with other varieties. Cage plants or bag blossoms to prevent cross-pollination.

ISOLATION DISTANCE: ¼ mile (0.4 km)

SEED MATURITY: Harvest capsules as soon as flowers are spent and before fruit shatters. Dry flower heads on screens.

SEED PROCESSING: Rub, flail

SEED VIABILITY: 2–4 years

Sweet Pea
Lathyrus odoratus

These old-fashioned, delicate beauties look gorgeous, both in the garden and in a vase. They need support as they're a vining plant, but the extra bit of work is worth it. Start them early, as sweet peas prefer cooler temperatures and fade in summer's heat. The old-fashioned, open-pollinated varieties are the ones with the amazing fragrance, which is a great reason to select heirloom varieties over hybrids as some hybrids are fragrance-free. Plus, you'll want to save seeds of these lovelies so you can grow them again and again in your garden.

NOTE: *All parts of the plant are poisonous.*

SWEET PEA

COMMON NAME: Sweet Pea

SCIENTIFIC NAME: *Lathyrus odoratus*

FAMILY: Fabaceae

LIFE CYCLE: Annual, perennial

USES: Cut flower, landscape, cottage garden, pollinators, attract hummingbirds, arbors, fences, trellises

FRUIT TYPE: Legumes (pods)

SEED-STARTING DEPTH: 1" (3 cm)

SPECIAL NEEDS: Scarify. Soak seeds 24 hours in water until the seeds are swollen. Needs dark to germinate.

SEED-STARTING SOIL TEMPERATURE: 55–65°F (13–18°C)

SEED START TIMING: Direct sowing 6 weeks before last frost is preferred. Can be started indoors using biodegradable containers 8–10 weeks before last frost.

LIGHT REQUIREMENTS: As soon as seedlings emerge

TRANSPLANT: Plant in full sun in rich, loamy, moist, well-drained soil after danger of frost. Do not disturb roots. Space 6" (15 cm) apart. Requires trellising. Pinch seedlings when they're 6–8" (15–20 cm) tall to encourage branching.

DIRECT SOWING: Sow 6 weeks prior to last frost.

GERMINATION: 14–21 days

DAYS TO MATURITY: 75–85

POLLINATION: Self, insect

CROSS-POLLINATION: Can cross-pollinate with other varieties. Cage plants or bag blossoms to prevent cross-pollination.

ISOLATION DISTANCE: 25' (8 m)

SEED MATURITY: Harvest pods when they're dry. Place pods on screens to dry for 1 month.

SEED PROCESSING: Flail

SEED VIABILITY: 3–5 years

Daisy
Leucanthemum spp.

The daisy is a forgiving plant that grows easily and spreads into large stands in a garden. Daisies represent innocence in the language of flowers, which is a perfect definition for their cheerful, friendly blooms. Pollinators love them, and they make a perfect, simple bouquet to add to the kitchen table. Cut a bunch of daisies, add them to a glass jar, and give them to your neighbor or friend. You'll see how daisies brighten everyone's day.

DAISY

COMMON NAME: Daisy

SCIENTIFIC NAME: *Leucanthemum* spp.

FAMILY: Asteraceae

LIFE CYCLE: Perennial

USES: Cut flower, cottage garden, landscape, pollinators, edible flower

FRUIT TYPE: Achene

SEED-STARTING DEPTH: Surface sow

SPECIAL NEEDS: It needs light to germinate.

SEED-STARTING SOIL TEMPERATURE: 65–75°F (18–24°C)

SEED START TIMING: Direct sow after frost. Can be started indoors 8–10 weeks before last frost. Bottom heat speeds germination.

LIGHT REQUIREMENTS: It needs light to germinate. As seedlings emerge, continue 12–16 hours of light per day.

TRANSPLANT: Plant in full sun in moist, well-drained, fertile soil after danger of frost. Space 18–24" (46–61 cm) apart.

DIRECT SOWING: Two weeks prior to last frost. Plants bloom the second year.

GERMINATION: 14–21 days

DAYS TO MATURITY: 90–120

POLLINATION: Insect

CROSS-POLLINATION: Can cross-pollinate with other varieties. Cage plants or bag blossoms to prevent cross-pollination.

ISOLATION DISTANCE: ½ mile (0.8 km)

SEED MATURITY: Harvest flower heads when they're brown and dry. Place on screens until completely dry.

SEED PROCESSING: Flail, rub

SEED VIABILITY: 3 years

Flax
Linum spp.

You'll find about two hundred species of flax, including *Linum usitatissimum*, the plant used for fiber in linen and the oil of flaxseed oil. However, most gardeners focus on the more ornamental varieties, such as *L. perenne* (perennial blue flax), and *L. grandiflorum* (scarlet flax). While each bloom only lasts for one day, flax will bloom continuously throughout the season, adding lovely color to your garden.

FLAX

COMMON NAME: Flax

SCIENTIFIC NAME: *Linum* spp.

FAMILY: *Linaceae*

LIFE CYCLE: Annual, perennial

USES: Fiber, oil, landscape, pollinators, culinary (seeds), medicinal

FRUIT TYPE: Capsule

SEED-STARTING DEPTH: ⅛" (0.3 cm)

SPECIAL NEEDS: Perennial varieties benefit from stratification.

SEED-STARTING SOIL TEMPERATURE: 70–75°F (21–24°C)

SEED START TIMING: Direct sowing after frost is preferred. Can be started indoors using biodegradable containers 7–8 weeks before last frost.

LIGHT REQUIREMENTS: As soon as seedlings emerge.

TRANSPLANT: Plant in full sun in well-drained soil after danger of frost. Do not disturb roots. Space 6" (15 cm) apart for smaller varieties, 12–24" (30–61 cm) apart for larger varieties.

DIRECT SOWING: Direct sow in late fall for natural stratification or in early spring after frost.

GERMINATION: 21–28 days

DAYS TO MATURITY: 70–100, depending on variety

POLLINATION: Insect

CROSS-POLLINATION: Can cross-pollinate with other varieties. Cage plants or bag blossoms to prevent cross-pollination.

ISOLATION DISTANCE: ¼ mile (0.4 km)

SEED MATURITY: Harvest when the flower head is dry and seeds are hard and dark in color.

SEED PROCESSING: Thresh, flail

SEED VIABILITY: 1–2 years

Alyssum
Lobularia maritima

If you like nearly instant gardening gratification, alyssum is for you. The darling petite flowers bloom only 6 weeks after sowing. In the language of flowers, alyssum symbolizes "worth beyond beauty," and the meaning is quite appropriate. Its worth stems from its ability to add a large impact to gardens, attracting pollinators with its sweet fragrance, while being low fuss and trouble-free.

ALYSSUM

COMMON NAMES: Alyssum, sweet alyssum, carpet flower

SCIENTIFIC NAME: *Lobularia maritima*

FAMILY: Brassicaceae

LIFE CYCLE: Annual (may be perennial in warmer climates)

USES: Borders, landscape, containers, companion plant, pollinators

FRUIT TYPE: Silicles

SEED-STARTING DEPTH: Surface sow

SPECIAL NEEDS: It needs light to germinate

SEED-STARTING SOIL TEMPERATURE: 55–70°F (13–21°C)

SEED START TIMING: Direct sow 2 weeks prior to last frost. Can be started indoors using biodegradable containers 6–8 weeks before last frost. Bottom heat speeds germination.

LIGHT REQUIREMENTS: It needs light to germinate. As seedlings emerge, continue 12–16 hours of light per day.

TRANSPLANT: Plant after danger of frost. Space 8–12" (20–30 cm) apart.

DIRECT SOWING: Direct sow 2 weeks prior to last frost.

GERMINATION: 14–21 days

DAYS TO MATURITY: 42–60

POLLINATION: Insect

CROSS-POLLINATION: Can cross-pollinate with other varieties. Cage plants or bag blossoms to prevent cross-pollination.

ISOLATION DISTANCE: ¼ mile (0.4 km)

SEED MATURITY: Seeds mature unevenly on plants and shatter easily. Hand harvest as silicles turn brown. Dry on screens with a sheet underneath to catch seeds.

SEED PROCESSING: Flail

SEED VIABILITY: 3–5 years

Stock
Matthiola spp.

With hundreds of varieties of stock available, it's easy to grow and add this fragrant flower to your borders or cutting garden. While it means "lasting beauty" in the language of flowers, stock actually prefers cooler spring temperatures and begins to fade in summer's heat. Start early to enjoy stock's lovely perfume.

·TRAITS AND TIPS·

STOCK

COMMON NAME: Stock

SCIENTIFIC NAME: *Matthiola* spp. (*M. incana*, *M. longipetala*, *M. sinuata*, *M. odorata*)

FAMILY: Brassicaceae

LIFE CYCLE: Annual, biennial

USES: Cut flower, landscape, cottage garden, companion plant, pollinators, edible flowers

FRUIT TYPE: Silique

SEED-STARTING DEPTH: ¼" (0.6 cm)

SPECIAL NEEDS: None

SEED-STARTING SOIL TEMPERATURE: 65–75°F (18–24°C)

SEED START TIMING: Start indoors using biodegradable containers 8–10 weeks before last frost. Bottom heat speeds germination.

LIGHT REQUIREMENTS: As soon as seedlings emerge

TRANSPLANT: Plant after danger of frost. Do not disturb roots. Don't allow plants to become rootbound, as it can stress the plants and cause them to bloom on shorter stems. Space 6" (15 cm) apart.

DIRECT SOWING: Sow after danger of frost has passed and when temperatures reach 55°F (13°C).

GERMINATION: 7–21 days

DAYS TO MATURITY: 90–105

POLLINATION: Insect

CROSS-POLLINATION: Can cross-pollinate with other varieties. Cage plants or bag blossoms to prevent cross-pollination.

ISOLATION DISTANCE: 25' (8 m)

SEED MATURITY: Harvest when fruits turn yellow-brown. Collect yellow seedpods by hand and dry on screen.

SEED PROCESSING: Thresh

SEED VIABILITY: 3–7 years

Bells of Ireland
Moluccella laevis

According to lore, this plant brings good fortune to gardeners. Whether or not bells of Ireland brings luck for you, it does add a great statement to the garden and to bouquets. An apple-green, bell-shaped calyx surrounds a small white flower. The plants add height in the garden and tolerate heat, but bells of Ireland doesn't enjoy humid climates. It does, however, last a full week as a cut flower in a vase.

·TRAITS AND TIPS·

BELLS OF IRELAND

COMMON NAMES: Bells of Ireland, shellflower

SCIENTIFIC NAME: *Moluccella laevis*

FAMILY: Lamiaceae

LIFE CYCLE: Annual

USES: Cut flower, dried flower, landscape, cottage garden, pollinators

FRUIT TYPE: Nutlet

SEED-STARTING DEPTH: Surface sow

SPECIAL NEEDS: Stratify at 50°F (10°C) for 5 days, then germinate at 50°F (10°C) at night, 85°F (29°C) during day. Use a heat mat to control temperatures. It needs light to germinate.

SEED-STARTING SOIL TEMPERATURE: 50–85°F (10–29°C). See above notes.

SEED START TIMING: Start indoors 6–8 weeks before last frost.

LIGHT REQUIREMENTS: It needs light to germinate. As seedlings emerge, continue 12–16 hours of light per day.

TRANSPLANT: Plant in full sun in well-drained soil after danger of frost. Space 12–15" (30–38 cm) apart. Needs staking. Does not enjoy hot, humid climates.

DIRECT SOWING: Sow after danger of frost has passed and when temperatures reach 55°F (13°C).

GERMINATION: 10–20 days

DAYS TO MATURITY: 90–110

POLLINATION: Insect

CROSS-POLLINATION: Can cross-pollinate with other varieties. Cage plants or bag blossoms to prevent cross-pollination.

ISOLATION DISTANCE: 300' (91m)

SEED MATURITY: Seeds are ready to harvest when nutlets dry. Harvest entire plants and place on screens to dry thoroughly. Wear gloves when harvesting.

SEED PROCESSING: Thresh, flail

SEED VIABILITY: 1 year

Love in a Mist
Nigella damascena

Popular since Elizabethan times for its delicate, asparagus fern–like foliage; beautiful pink, blue, and white blooms; and interesting seedpods, love in a mist is an easy seed to start and save. Legend ties love in a mist to the Roman Emperor Frederick I Barbarossa, who drowned in the Saleph River while leading a crusade through Turkey. According to the story, a water sprite lured him into the river, where he died. On the shore, a *Nigella* bloom appeared, representing his departed spirit.

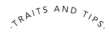

LOVE IN A MIST

COMMON NAMES: Love in a mist, devil in a bush, ragged lady

SCIENTIFIC NAME: *Nigella damascena*

FAMILY: Ranunculaceae

LIFE CYCLE: Annual

USES: Landscape, companion plant, containers, cottage garden, meadow, cut flower, dried flower, pollinators

FRUIT TYPE: Follicle

SEED-STARTING DEPTH: ⅛" (0.3 cm)

SPECIAL NEEDS: None

SEED-STARTING SOIL TEMPERATURE: 65–70°F (18–21°C)

SEED START TIMING: Direct sowing in fall is preferred. Can be started indoors using biodegradable containers 6–8 weeks before last frost.

LIGHT REQUIREMENTS: As soon as seedlings emerge

TRANSPLANT: Plant in full sun, part shade after danger of frost. Do not disturb roots. Space 6" (15 cm) apart.

DIRECT SOWING: Direct sow in fall in mild climates, or sow in spring after danger of frost when soil temperatures reach 60°F (16°C).

GERMINATION: 7–14 days

DAYS TO MATURITY: 65–70 for flowers, 75–80 for seedpods

POLLINATION: Insect

CROSS-POLLINATION: Can cross-pollinate with other varieties. Cage plants or bag blossoms to prevent cross-pollination.

ISOLATION DISTANCE: ¼ mile (0.4 km)

SEED MATURITY: Harvest when the plant follicles are dry. Spread fruits on screens to dry fully.

SEED PROCESSING: Flail, rub

SEED VIABILITY: 2–5 years

Poppy
Papaver spp.

With approximately one hundred species of poppies, it's a little tricky to know which varieties to grow. Before you venture into adding *Papaver somniferum*, the infamous opium poppy, to your garden, make certain you know the law. It's illegal to process the poppy to make drugs, of course, but there's conflicting information about growing the plant for flowers and the culinary use of its seeds. Instead, perhaps stick with safe alternatives, such as Shirley, the poppy of Flanders Fields fame, or the stunning Iceland poppies popular with florists.

·TRAITS AND TIPS·

POPPY

COMMON NAME: Poppy

SCIENTIFIC NAMES: *Papaver* spp.
P. somniferum (pompom, opium)—annual

P. rhoeas (Shirley, famous for Flanders Fields)—annual
P. orientale (Oriental)—perennial
P. nudicaule (Iceland)—biennial
Eschsoholzia californica (California poppy)—annual

FAMILY: Papaveraceae

LIFE CYCLE: Annual, perennial, or biennial

USES: Cut flower, landscape, pollinators, cottage garden, meadow, dried flower (seedhead)

FRUIT TYPE: Capsule

SEED-STARTING DEPTH: Perennial, surface sow; annual, ¼" (0.6 cm) (needs dark to germinate)

SPECIAL NEEDS: Perennials need light to germinate; annuals need dark to germinate. Some varieties, like *P. radicatum* and *P. burseri,* benefit from stratification.

SEED-STARTING SOIL TEMPERATURE: Perennial 68–70°F (20–21°C); annual 60°F (16°C)

SEED START TIMING: Direct sow in fall or early spring. Can be started indoors using biodegradable containers 6–8 weeks before last frost.

LIGHT REQUIREMENTS: As soon as seedlings emerge. Perennials need light to germinate.

TRANSPLANT: Plant after danger of frost. Do not disturb roots. Space 8–12" (20–30 cm) apart.

DIRECT SOWING: Sowing is preferred after danger of frost has passed and when soil temperatures reach 55°F (13°C). Can direct sow in fall in mild climates.

GERMINATION: 21–28 days

DAYS TO MATURITY: 90–120 annuals (flowers the first year); perennials (blooms the second year).

POLLINATION: Insect

CROSS-POLLINATION: Can cross-pollinate with other varieties. Cage plants or bag blossoms to prevent cross-pollination.

ISOLATION DISTANCE: 300' (91 m)

SEED MATURITY: Dry capsules on plants or harvest entire plants prior to frost. Allow capsules to continue to dry fully on screens.

SEED PROCESSING: Shake fruits over a bag or container to extract seeds.

SEED VIABILITY: 3 years

Passion Flower Vine
Passiflora spp.

Passion flower vine is one of my favorite plants to grow from seed. While it takes until the second year to bloom, the flowers are worth the wait. Its unique, tropical-like bloom attracts pollinators, the vine grows quickly to cover trellises and fences, and it serves as a host plant for several butterfly species' larvae. Oh, and depending on the variety (there are more than four hundred), you may get edible fruit too. Make sure you add passion flower vine to your list of seeds to grow.

PASSION FLOWER VINE

COMMON NAMES: Passion flower vine, passionflower, passionvine, maypop

SCIENTIFIC NAME: *Passiflora* spp.

FAMILY: Passifloraceae

LIFE CYCLE: Annual, perennial

USES: Culinary, medicinal, landscape, fences, trellises, arbors, pollinators, attracts hummingbirds, host plant for gulf fritillary and zebra long wing butterfly larvae

FRUIT TYPE: Berry

SEED-STARTING DEPTH: Surface sow

SPECIAL NEEDS: Scarify and soak seeds 1–2 days. It needs light for germination.

SEED-STARTING SOIL TEMPERATURE: 65–75°F (18–24°C)

SEED START TIMING: Start indoors using biodegradable containers 10–12 weeks before last frost. Bottom heat speeds germination.

LIGHT REQUIREMENTS: It needs light to germinate. As seedlings emerge, continue 12–16 hours of light per day.

TRANSPLANT: Plant in full sun or part shade in rich, loamy, well-drained soil after danger of frost. Do not disturb roots. Space 8–12" (20–30 cm) apart. Requires trellising, as vines can reach 15–20' (5–6 m) in length.

DIRECT SOWING: Sow after danger of frost and when temperatures reach 55°F (13°C).

GERMINATION: 10–20 days

DAYS TO MATURITY: 60–80, depending on variety. Perennials bloom second year.

POLLINATION: Insect

CROSS-POLLINATION: Can cross-pollinate with other varieties. Cage plants or bag blossoms to prevent cross-pollination.

ISOLATION DISTANCE: ½ mile (0.8 km)

MATURITY: Harvest fully ripe fruit and open the pods to remove seeds.

SEED PROCESSING: Rinse and dry

SEED VIABILITY: 1 year

Phlox
Phlox spp.

From the Greek word meaning "flame," phlox range from short, creeping groundcovers that appear in early spring to tall, billowy garden blooms perfect for bouquets. With more than sixty species of annual and perennial phlox, they serve many purposes in the garden. Pollinators adore the blooms, the shorter varieties make excellent borders and perfect additions to rock gardens, and the taller species add lovely color to landscapes and cutting gardens.

PHLOX

COMMON NAMES: Phlox, garden phlox, creeping phlox

SCIENTIFIC NAMES: *Phlox* spp. (*P. drummondii*, annual; *P. divaricate*, perennial woodland phlox; *P. paniculata*, perennial garden phlox)

FAMILY: Polemoniaceae

LIFE CYCLE: Annual, perennial

USES: Landscape, groundcover, cottage garden, pollinators, companion plant, cut flower

FRUIT TYPE: Capsule

SEED-STARTING DEPTH: ⅛" (0.3 cm)

SPECIAL NEEDS: Stratify perennials for 4 weeks. Annuals need dark to germinate.

SEED-STARTING SOIL TEMPERATURE: 60–65°F (16–18°C)

SEED START TIMING: Direct sowing after frost is preferred. Can be started indoors using biodegradable containers 4–6 weeks before last frost.

LIGHT REQUIREMENTS: As soon as seedlings emerge

TRANSPLANT: Plant in full or part sun in loamy, well-drained soil after danger of frost. Do not disturb roots. Space 8" (20 cm) apart for annuals, 12" (30 cm) for perennials.

DIRECT SOWING: Sow after danger of frost has passed and when temperatures reach 55°F (13°C).

GERMINATION: 5–10 days

DAYS TO MATURITY: 50 to 65 (annuals); perennials flower the second year.

POLLINATION: Insect

CROSS-POLLINATION: Can cross-pollinate with other varieties. Cage plants or bag blossoms to prevent cross-pollination.

ISOLATION DISTANCE: ½ mile (0.8 km)

SEED MATURITY: Harvest when capsules start to turn brown. Spread capsules on screen with sheet beneath to catch seeds to dry fully.

SEED PROCESSING: Flail, rub

SEED VIABILITY: 1–3 years

Black-Eyed Susan
Rudbeckia spp.

Rudbeckia is the champion of the late-summer garden. When the rest of the garden succumbs to summer's scorching temperatures and drought, you can count on the bright, tough blooms of black-eyed Susan to save the day. It tolerates heat and drought without complaint, and as the blooms fade as winter nears, the seedheads provide natural bird feeders. Make sure to bag some dried flowers to save seeds for next year's garden before the wildlife cleans you out. A word of caution: *Rudbeckia* species can be invasive in some areas. Check before planting.

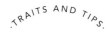

BLACK-EYED SUSAN

COMMON NAMES: Black-eyed Susan, brown Betty, brown-eyed Susan, yellow daisy, gloriosa daisy

SCIENTIFIC NAME: *Rudbeckia* spp.

FAMILY: Asteraceae

LIFE CYCLE: Tender perennial and annual

USES: Cut flower, landscape, pollinators, companion plant, meadow, cottage garden

FRUIT TYPE: Achene

SEED-STARTING DEPTH: Surface sow

SPECIAL NEEDS: Stratify for 3 weeks. It needs light to germinate.

SEED-STARTING SOIL TEMPERATURE: 68–72°F (20–22°C)

SEED START TIMING: Direct sowing 2 weeks before last frost is preferred. Can be started indoors using biodegradable containers 8–10 weeks before last frost. Bottom heat speeds germination.

LIGHT REQUIREMENTS: It needs light to germinate. As seedlings emerge, continue 12–16 hours of light per day. Space 12–18" (30–46 cm) apart.

DIRECT SOWING: Sow 2 weeks prior to last frost.

GERMINATION: 5–21 days

DAYS TO MATURITY: 90–105

POLLINATION: Insect

CROSS-POLLINATION: Can cross-pollinate with other varieties. Cage plants or bag blossoms to prevent cross-pollination.

ISOLATION DISTANCE: ¼ mile (0.4 km)

SEED MATURITY: Seeds are mature when the flowers dry. Collect seedheads by hand. Dry fully on screens.

SEED PROCESSING: Flail, rub (wear gloves)

SEED VIABILITY: 2 years

Marigold
Tagetes spp.

I start hundreds of marigolds every spring, from French marigolds to use as companion plants in the vegetable garden to African marigolds to add to bouquets. With more than fifty species, there are plenty of varieties from which to choose. Pollinators love them, and in the heat of summer, when other blooms melt and fade, marigolds still shine in the garden. Plus, they're quick to start from seed, and saving seed at the end of the season is simple.

MARIGOLD

COMMON NAMES: Marigold, African marigold, Mexican marigold, French marigold

SCIENTIFIC NAMES: *Tagetes* spp.; *T. patula* (French marigold); *T. erecta nana* (African marigold)

FAMILY: Asteraceae

LIFE CYCLE: Annual and perennial

USES: Landscape, borders, cut flower, companion plant, containers, dried flower, pollinators, culinary, dyes

FRUIT TYPE: Achenes

SEED-STARTING DEPTH: Surface sow

SPECIAL NEEDS: It needs light to germinate.

SEED-STARTING SOIL TEMPERATURE: 70–75°F (21–24°C)

SEED START TIMING: Direct sow after frost. Can be started indoors 6–8 weeks before last frost. Bottom heat speeds germination.

LIGHT REQUIREMENTS: As soon as seedlings emerge

TRANSPLANT: Plant in full sun in fertile, well-drained soil after danger of frost. Space 8–10" (20–25 cm) apart for smaller varieties, 10–12" (25–30 cm) apart for tall varieties.

DIRECT SOWING: Sow after danger of frost has passed and when soil temperatures reach 60°F (16°C).

GERMINATION: 3–14 days

DAYS TO MATURITY: 50 to 80, depending on variety

POLLINATION: Self, insect

CROSS-POLLINATION: Can cross-pollinate with other varieties. Cage plants or bag blossoms to prevent cross-pollination

ISOLATION DISTANCE: ¼ mile (0.4 km)

SEED MATURITY: Cut off dried blooms or pull the entire plant and let it dry completely when flowering ends.

SEED PROCESSING: Flail, then dry seeds an additional week before storing.

SEED VIABILITY: 3–5 years

Mexican Sunflower
Tithonia rotundifolia

The bright, showy blooms of *Tithonia* cheerfully beckon to pollinators in the summer and fall, glowing in the garden while many of the other blooms look sad and bedraggled. A native of Mexico and Central America, Mexican sunflower thrives in the heat. Named for Tithonus, the Prince of Troy who fell in love with the dawn goddess Aurora, the blooms resemble the orange glow of dawn.

MEXICAN SUNFLOWER

COMMON NAME: Mexican sunflower

SCIENTIFIC NAME: *Tithonia rotundifolia*

FAMILY: Asteraceae

LIFE CYCLE: Annual

USES: Cut flower, landscape, cottage garden, meadow, pollinators, companion plant

FRUIT TYPE: Achenes

SEED-STARTING DEPTH: Surface sow

SPECIAL NEEDS: It needs light to germinate.

SEED-STARTING SOIL TEMPERATURE: 70–75°F (21–24°C)

SEED START TIMING: Direct sow after frost. Can be started indoors 6–8 weeks before last frost. Bottom heat speeds germination.

LIGHT REQUIREMENTS: It needs light to germinate. As seedlings emerge, continue 12–16 hours of light per day.

TRANSPLANT: Plant in full sun after danger of frost. Space 18–24" (46–61 cm) apart. Once established, it tolerates dry conditions. May need staking in windy areas.

DIRECT SOWING: Sow after danger of frost has passed and when soil temperatures reach 60°F (16°C).

GERMINATION: 5–14 days

DAYS TO MATURITY: 85–90

POLLINATION: Insect

CROSS-POLLINATION: Can cross-pollinate with other varieties. Cage plants or bag blossoms to prevent cross-pollination.

ISOLATION DISTANCE: ½ mile (0.8 km)

SEED MATURITY: Dry flowers on plants or harvest prior to frost. Allow flower heads to dry thoroughly.

SEED PROCESSING: Thresh, flail

SEED VIABILITY: 2–3 years

Nasturtium
Tropaeolum majus

From their beautiful blooms to their umbrella-shaped foliage, which is sometimes variegated, nasturtiums belong in every garden. Tuck them into vegetable beds for companion plantings. Trellis them on arbors, particularly the tall varieties such as 'Phoenix'. Fill containers with them to add beauty to your balcony. But whatever you do, grow them. They're easy to start from seed, provide a tasty treat, whether you're using the peppery blooms in salads or pickling the flower buds and seedpods like capers, and they add beauty to the landscape.

NASTURTIUM

COMMON NAMES: Nasturtium, Indian cress

SCIENTIFIC NAME: *Tropaeolum majus*

FAMILY: Tropaeolaceae

LIFE CYCLE: Perennial and annual

USES: Landscape, borders, containers, companion plant, medicinal, pollinators, culinary (all parts of the plant are edible)

FRUIT TYPE: Schizocarp

SEED-STARTING DEPTH: ½" (1.3 cm)

SPECIAL NEEDS: Scarify and soak seeds in water overnight. It needs dark to germinate.

SEED-STARTING SOIL TEMPERATURE: 60–65°F (16–18°C)

SEED START TIMING: Direct sow 2 weeks before last frost. Can be started indoors using biodegradable containers 4–6 weeks before last frost.

LIGHT REQUIREMENTS: As soon as seedlings emerge

TRANSPLANT: Plant in full sun to part shade after danger of frost. Do not disturb roots. Space 8–12" (20–30 cm) apart. Plant 3–5 plants in a 10"-diameter (25 cm) basket. Some varieties need trellising.

DIRECT SOWING: Sow seeds 2 weeks prior to last frost.

GERMINATION: 7–10 days

DAYS TO MATURITY: 55–65

POLLINATION: Insect

CROSS-POLLINATION: Can cross-pollinate with other varieties. Cage plants or bag blossoms to prevent cross-pollination.

ISOLATION DISTANCE: ¼ mile (0.4 km)

SEED MATURITY: Dry on the vines and collect by hand or harvest entire flowers and allow seeds to continue to dry fully.

SEED PROCESSING: Hand, flail

SEED VIABILITY: 3–5 years

Pansy
Viola spp.

With hundreds of varieties available today, the pansy is steeped in history. A posy of pansies in Victorian days meant that your admirer was thinking of you, as the name "pansy" originates from the French word *pense*, meaning *thought*. However, some of its lore isn't quite so pleasant, as a pansy picked while the dew was still fresh would lead to the death of a loved one, according to legend. And it was believed that if pansies bloom in autumn, plague would follow.

·TRAITS AND TIPS·

PANSY

COMMON NAMES: Pansy, viola, Johnny jump up

SCIENTIFIC NAMES: *Viola* spp. *(V. tricolor* Johnny Jump Up)

FAMILY: Violaceae

LIFE CYCLE: Annual, biennial, perennial

USES: Landscape, containers, pollinators, borders, companion plant, culinary (edible flowers)

FRUIT TYPE: Capsule

SEED-STARTING DEPTH: Surface sow

SPECIAL NEEDS: Stratify 2 weeks to increase germination.

SEED-STARTING SOIL TEMPERATURE: 62–68°F (17–20°C)

SEED START TIMING: Start indoors 10–12 weeks before last frost.

LIGHT REQUIREMENTS: As soon as seedlings emerge

TRANSPLANT: Plant in full sun to part shade after danger of frost. Space 6–10" (15–25 cm) apart.

DIRECT SOWING: Not recommended

GERMINATION: 4–15 days

DAYS TO MATURITY: 60–90, depending on variety

POLLINATION: Self, insect

CROSS-POLLINATION: Can cross-pollinate with other varieties. Cage plants or bag blossoms to prevent cross-pollination.

ISOLATION DISTANCE: 600' (183 m)

SEED MATURITY: Handpick fruits as flowers dry. Place on screens to dry completely with a sheet underneath to catch seeds.

SEED PROCESSING: Thresh

SEED VIABILITY: 2–3 years

Zinnia
Zinnia spp.

One of the most prolific, easiest plants to grow from seed, zinnias are worth trying in your garden. With exuberant colors and drought tolerance, zinnias make the perfect plant for the summer garden, attracting pollinators while also providing cheerful blooms for bouquets. In the language of flowers, zinnias represent "thoughts of absent friends." Snip a few blooms and leave a little bouquet on a friend's porch as a summer surprise to let them know you're thinking of them.

ZINNIA

COMMON NAME: Zinnia

SCIENTIFIC NAMES: *Zinnia* spp. (*Z. elegans,* common zinnia; *Z. haageana,* Mexican zinnia; *Z. peruviana,* Peruvian zinnia)

FAMILY: Asteraceae

LIFE CYCLE: Annual

USES: Cut flower, landscape, companion plant, pollinators, containers, cottage garden, borders

FRUIT TYPE: Achenes

SEED-STARTING DEPTH: ¼" (0.6 cm)

SPECIAL NEEDS: Bottom heat speeds germination.

SEED-STARTING SOIL TEMPERATURE: 75–85°F (24–29°C)

SEED START TIMING: Direct sow after frost or start indoors using biodegradable containers 6–8 weeks before last frost. Bottom heat speeds germination.

LIGHT REQUIREMENTS: As soon as seedlings emerge

TRANSPLANT: Plant in full sun in rich, well-drained soil after danger of frost. Do not disturb roots, and don't allow plants to become rootbound. Space 9–12" (23–30 cm) apart.

DIRECT SOWING: Sow after danger of frost has passed and when soil temperatures reach 65°F (18°C).

GERMINATION: 3–5 days

DAYS TO MATURITY: 75–90

POLLINATION: Insect

CROSS-POLLINATION: Can cross-pollinate with other varieties. Cage plants or bag blossoms to prevent cross-pollination.

ISOLATION DISTANCE: ½ mile (0.8 km)

SEED MATURITY: Harvest individual flowers heads as they dry. Keep flower heads dry before harvest. Spread on a screen to dry fully. Note: do not harvest seeds on plants with powdery mildew.

SEED PROCESSING: Flail

SEED VIABILITY: 3–5 years

Acknowledgments

Gardeners are the most generous people I know. From sharing seeds to offering advice, some of my closest friends are those with dirt under their nails. I'm grateful for my tribe of talented, tenacious gardeners, garden writers, farmers, and horticulture professionals. Thank you all for your wisdom, pass-along plants, laughter, and support.

Some of these gardening champions graciously allowed us to tramp through their gardens in pursuit of photos as fall and winter crept into my garden. Thank you to the folks at Sunny Point Café in Asheville, North Carolina, and Charleston Parks Conservancy, Middleton Place Organic Farm, and Compost in My Shoe in Charleston, South Carolina.

My fabulous friend and photographer Libby Williams, owner of Libby Williams Photographs, created magic when garden pickings were slim. She can also add "therapist" to her resume, because Libby provided an oasis of calm when I fretted over finding produce in November or blooms in January. If you need a photographer, Libby makes all things beautiful.

I'm also grateful to my editor, Thom O'Hearn, who stepped into the project and calmed a new author's anxieties.

A big thank you to my family for not imploding while I spent hours writing at the kitchen table, or more hours pampering the green babies instead of my human ones. Our daughter, Kristen, performed beautifully as a substitute algebra tutor and chauffeur for Michael while I was busy with the book (or pretending to be, so I wouldn't have to tackle math). We're lucky to have fabulous kids.

My husband, Peter, is my biggest cheerleader. He believes in me even when impostor syndrome rears its ugly head. Peter built my greenhouses, ignores seedlings spread throughout the house, and always makes my crazy garden ideas work, although he'd rather be sailing. I owe him serious crew time after all of the garden work he's logged.

And, finally, thank you to all the champions of heirlooms: the families who've shared seeds, the farmers who grow the plants and ensure pure seeds, and the companies that make them available to us so we can enjoy them in our gardens.

Credits

Libby Williams: cover, 1, 2, 3, 6, 10, 12, 13, 15 (top), 16, 17, 19, 23, 24, 25, 26, 28, 29, 31, 33, 34, 35, 36, 37, 39, 41, 42, 46, 48, 51, 52, 53, 54, 58, 59, 61, 63, 64, 65, 66, 67, 76, 77, 79, 84 (bottom), 88, 89, 90, 91, 94, 95, 104, 107, 113, 114, 115, 117, 121, 122, 133, 135, 138, 146, 147, 149, 150

Julie Thompson-Adolf: 21, 49, 69, 99, 103, 108, 112, 132, 136, 137, 148

Shutterstock: 7, 11, 14, 15 (bottom), 18, 22, 38, 45, 50, 72, 84 (top), 85, 86, 87, 92, 98, 100, 109, 111, 125, 128, 143, 144

Resources

Seeds/Seed-Starting and -Saving Supplies

UNITED STATES

Baker Creek Heirloom Seeds	www.rareseeds.com
Botanical Interests	www.botanicalinterests.com
Burpee	www.burpee.com
Eden Brothers	www.edenbrothers.com
Fedco Seeds	www.fedcoseeds.com
Floret Flowers	www.floretflowers.com
J. W. Jung Seed Company	www.jungseed.com
Johnny's Selected Seeds	www.johnnyseeds.com
Harris Seeds	www.harrisseeds.com
Heirloom Seeds	www.heirloomseeds.com
High Mowing Organic Seeds	www.highmowingseeds.com
Kitazawa Seed Company	www.kitazawaseed.com
Monticello	www.monticelloshop.org
Nichols Garden Nursery	www.nicholsgardennursery.com
Peaceful Valley Farm & Garden Supply	www.groworganic.com
Pinetree Garden Seeds	www.superseeds.com
Renee's Garden	www.reneesgarden.com
The Seed Keeper Company	www.seedkeeper.com
Seed Savers Exchange	www.seedsavers.org
Seeds from Italy	www.growitalian.com
Seeds 'n Such	www.seedsnsuch.com
Seeds of Change	www.seedsofchange.com
Select Seeds	www.selectseeds.com
Southern Exposure Seed Exchange	ww.southernexposure.com
Strictly Medicinal Seeds	www.strictlymedicinalseeds.com
Sustainable Seed Company	www.sustainableseedco.com
Territorial Seed Company	www.territorialseed.com
Victory Seeds	www.victoryseeds.com
West Coast Seeds	www.westcoastseeds.com

INTERNATIONAL

Arcoiris (Italy)	www.arcoiris.it
Fratelli Ingegnoli (Italy)	www.ingegnoli.it/ita
Halifax Seed (Canada)	www.halifaxseed.ca
Heritage Harvest Seed (Canada)	www.heritageharvestseed.com
The Real Seed Catalog (UK)	www.realseeds.co.uk
Richters (Canada)	www.richters.com
Salt Spring Seeds (Canada)	www.saltspringseeds.com
The Seed Company (Canada)	www.theseedcompany.ca
Stokes Seeds (Canada)	www.stokeseeds.com
Terra Edibles (Canada)	www.terraedibles.ca
Wildflower Farm (Canada)	www.wildflowerfarm.com

SEED-SAVING ORGANIZATIONS

Global Seed Network	www.globalseednetwork.org
Hawaii Seed	www.hawaiiseed.org
International Seed Saving Institute	www.seedsave.org
Navdanya	www.navdanya.org
Open Source Seed Initiative	www.osseeds.org
Organic Seed Alliance	www.seedalliance.org
Organic Seed Growers and Trade Association	www.osgata.org
Rocky Mountain Seed Alliance	www.rockymountainseeds.org
The Seed Ambassadors Project	www.seedambassadors.org
Seed Savers Exchange	www.seedsavers.org
Slow Food International	www.slowfood.com
Svalbard Global Seed Vault	www.croptrust.org/our-work/svalbard-global-seed-vault

Index

A

Abelmoschus esculentus, 59
Achillea millefoliu, 99–100
Allium ampeloprasum, 60
Allium schoenoprasum, 100–101
Allium tuberosum, 100–101
Almutaster, 126–127
Alyssum, 140
Anethum graveolens, 101–102
Anthriscus cerefolium, 102–103
Antirrhinum majus, 123
Apium graveolens, 61–62
Aquilegia spp., 123–124
Artichoke, 74–75
Arugula, 77
Asclepias spp., 124–125
Asparagus, 62–63
Aspargus officinalis, 62–63
Aster, 126–127
Aster amellus, 126–127

B

Bachelor's buttons, 129–130
Bagging, 47
Basil, 114–115
Bean, 80–82
Bee balm, 113–114
Beets, 64–65
Belgian endive, 70–71
Bellflower, 127
Bells of Ireland, 141–142
Beta vulgaris, 64–65
Black-eyed Susan, 146
Blanket flower, 134
Borage, 103–104
Borago officinalis, 103–104
Brassicas, 66–68
Broccoli, 66–68
Broccoli raab, 66–68
Brussels sprouts, 66–68

C

Cabbage, 66–68
Caging, 48–49
Calendula, 104–105
Calendula officinalis, 104–105
Callistephus chinensis, 126–127
Campanula, 127
Canadanthus, 126–127
Capsicum spp., 68–70
Cardiospermum halicabum, 127–128
Cardoon, 74–75
Carrot, 75–76
Cauliflower, 66–68
Celery/celeriac, 61–62
Celosia, 129
Celosia spp., 129
Centaurea cyanus, 129–130
Chamaemelum nobile, 105
Chamomile, 105
Chervil, 102–103
Chinese broccoli, 66–68
Chinese cabbage, 66–68
Chive, 100–101
Choosing seeds, 18–19, 20–21
Cicer arietinum, 80–82
Cichorium endivia, 70–71
Cichorium intybus, 70–71
Cilantro, 106
Citron melon, 71–72
Citrullus lanatus, 71–72
Cleome, 130
Cleome hassleriana, 130
Cockscomb, 129
Collards, 66–68
Columbine, 123–124
Compost, 43
Coneflower, 107–108
Conventional seeds, 20–21
Coreopsis, 131
Coreopsis spp., 131
Coriander, 106
Coriandrum sativum, 106
Corn, 96–97
Cornflowers, 129–130
Cosmos, 131–132
Cosmos bipinnatus, 131–132

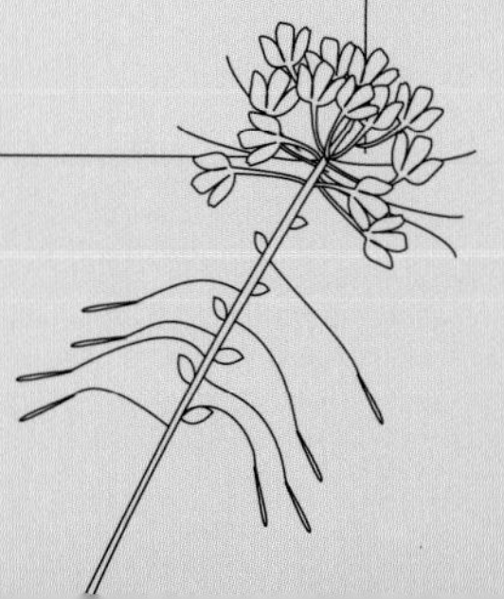

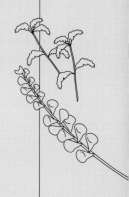

About the Author

Julie Thompson-Adolf is an obsessive organic gardener, nature nut, ecoadventurer, animal advocate, and seed lover. As an experienced gardener and garden writer, Julie is best known for her brand and blog, Garden Delights. She practices a seed-to-table-to-seed approach, starting her plants from seeds, creating delicious meals and beautiful bouquets from the harvest, and saving seeds to plant in next year's garden. Julie's suburban microfarm is often a site for tours and teaching. She is a master gardener, has served on the National Garden Bureau's Plant Nerds team, and joined with P. Allen Smith for Garden2Blog. Julie is a member of the Garden Writers Association, Slow Food, Carolina Farm Stewardship Association, and many other environmental and gardening groups. You can follow her garden, environmental, and travel writing on any of the major social media platforms:

BLOG
Garden Delights (juliesgardendelights.com)

FACEBOOK
Garden Delights

TWITTER
@garden_delights

INSTAGRAM
@juliesgardendelights

GOOGLE+
Julie Adolf